UNDERSTANDING MORTGAGES AND HOME EQUITY LOANS

Read this No Nonsense Guide if you want to know:

★ How mortgages work

★ All about houses, condominiums and co-ops

★ Which mortgage is the best for you

★ How to make the best use of the investment you have in your house

THE NO NONSENSE LIBRARY

NO NONSENSE FINANCIAL GUIDES

How to Finance Your Child's College Education
How to Use Credit and Credit Cards, Revised Edition
Understanding Tax-Exempt Bonds, Revised Edition
Understanding Money Market Funds, Revised Edition
Understanding Mutual Funds, Revised Edition
Understanding IRA's
Understanding Common Stocks, Revised Edition
Understanding Treasury Bills and Other U.S. Government Securities, Revised Edition
Understanding the Stock Market, Revised Edition
Understanding Stock Options and Futures Markets, Revised Edition
How to Choose a Discount Stockbroker, Revised Edition
How to Make Personal Financial Planning Work for You
How to Plan and Invest for Your Retirement
The New Tax Law and What It Means to You

NO NONSENSE REAL ESTATE GUIDES

Understanding Condominiums and Co-ops, Revised Edition
Understanding Buying and Selling a House, Revised Edition
Understanding Mortgages and Home Equity Loans, Revised Edition
Refinancing Your Mortgage, Revised Edition

NO NONSENSE LEGAL GUIDES

Understanding Estate Planning and Wills, Revised Edition
How to Choose A Lawyer

NO NONSENSE CAREER GUIDES

How to Use Your Time Wisely
Managing People: At Work, At Home

NO NONSENSE SUCCESS GUIDES

NO NONSENSE HEALTH GUIDES

NO NONSENSE COOKING GUIDES

NO NONSENSE WINE GUIDES

UNDERSTANDING MORTGAGES AND HOME EQUITY LOANS

Revised Edition

Phyllis C. Kaufman
& Arnold Corrigan

LONGMEADOW PRESS

To
Billy Wilson,
With love and thanks

The authors want to thank real estate developer and lecturer Jack W. Blumenfeld, without whose advice, help, and wisdom this book would not have been possible.

We are also grateful to the nationwide mortgage brokerage firm GMAC Mortgage Corporation, and especially to Elizabeth K. Muhr, Assistant Vice President, GMAC Mortgage Corporation of Pennsylvania.

This publication is designed to provide accurate and authoritative information with regard to the subject matter covered. It is sold with the understanding that neither the publisher nor the authors are engaged in rendering legal, accounting, or other professional services regarding the subject matter covered. If legal advice or other expert assistance is desired, the services of a competent professional person should be sought.

Understanding Mortgages, Revised Edition.

Cover art by Bets, Ltd.
Production services by William S. Konecky Associates, New York.

ISBN: 0-681-40246-6

Printed in the United States of America

0 9 8 7 6 5 4 3 2 1

CONTENTS

1

INTRODUCTION

The comfort and security of owning a home is a big part of the American Dream.

But the price of housing today makes it virtually impossible to save enough to pay cash for a home. Nor would you want to.

Historically, the American credit system has been shaped to help people borrow money for long periods to buy homes. U.S. financial institutions offer a tremendous quantity and variety of mortgage loans for home buyers; this system has no equal anywhere else in the world.

If you hesitate to borrow, even for the purpose of buying a home, stop worrying. You'll be pleased to know that when you assume the responsibility of a mortgage loan, your credit rating rises. You become a more financially responsible citizen.

However, the search for a mortgage can be a confusing and frustrating experience because of the many different types of loans available. This book will take you through the steps in mortgage hunting. You will learn which type of mortgage is best for you, and the ins and outs of refinancing and second mortgages.

The No Nonsense Real Estate Guide, *Understanding Mortgages*, will give you practical help in making the American Dream a reality.

2

WHAT IS A MORTGAGE?

We all use the word *mortgage* for convenience when in fact we are talking about a *mortgage loan*. The mortgage itself is not a loan, but a *pledge*. This makes sense once you understand how a mortgage actually works. When we speak about "getting a mortgage," we actually mean the *mortgage loan*. A bank or other lender lends you the money for your purchase and in return you give the lender a mortgage (pledge); you have pledged your property as security for the repayment of the loan, plus any interest that has accrued on it.

The lender then registers your pledge with the appropriate local authority in the form of a *lien*. A lien is a legal notice that if the property is sold or you fail to repay on schedule, the lien holder (lender) has a legal means, called foreclosure, of taking possession of the property in order to be repaid the amount owed.

Once the loan plus the interest has been paid off, the lien is removed and the pledged property is yours free and clear.

Who's Who

Let's look at the parties involved in the mortgage. You, the buyer of the property, are the borrower. You are the one who gives the mortgage (as your pledge for repayment), so you are called the *mortgagor*, the one who is mortgaging (pledging) the property. The lender of the money receives the mortgage pledge and is the *mortgagee*.

This word usage may seem to be in reverse. But when you remember that the mortgage is actually the pledge and not the loan, it makes perfect sense.

3

HOW DOES A MORTGAGE WORK?

Who Owns What

When you receive a mortgage loan, say from your present bank, and you go to settlement (closing) on your home purchase, the bank actually gives you a check for the face amount of the mortgage loan and you hand it over for payment to the seller together with your down payment.

Next, the title to the property is recorded in your name on the deed, and the mortgage lender records its lien with the appropriate local authority. What does this mean? It means that if you fail to make your payments each month as they become due, the bank can foreclose on the property—that is, the lender can, if it wishes, go to court to take over the property and sell it. When the property is sold, the money the bank is owed is paid to it from the proceeds of the sale, and you (the former owner) receive anything that is left over after all the costs are paid. If it's sold for less, you may still be liable for the balance, depending on the laws of your state.

If you go bankrupt, your mortgage lender is in a better position than your other creditors. The lien that the lender has filed on your property because of the mortgage loan becomes a first right against the property, and the lender gets paid off from the sale of the property before any of your other creditors, except the tax collector.

You should note that in some states, a Deed of Trust is used instead of a mortgage. A Deed of Trust is similar to a mortgage except that the borrower deeds the property to a trustee as guarantee of repayment.

3

4

A BIT OF HISTORY

In order to understand the present state of mortgage lending, you must understand something of its history.

Traditionally, mortgages were fixed-rate instruments that matured in anywhere from 15 to 30 years. You paid the same amount each and every month for the life of the loan.

The lending institution, whether it was a commercial bank, a savings and loan association or a credit union, would issue the loan, pay the principal to the seller of the house on your behalf, and collect the principal and interest back from you monthly.

The Rise in Interest Rates

Problems began in the 1970s when interest rates began to soar and mortgage interest rates went through the ceiling. By 1980–81, interest rates of 15%, 17%, even 18% were commonplace.

The financial institutions that were holding old mortgages at rates of 5% and 7% suffered. They were collecting money at low interest rates on old mortgages while they had to borrow money at the new higher rates in order to conduct business. The problem was enormous. A few lenders went bankrupt, many went out of business, and the financial industry realized that a change had to be made in the mortgage situation. And change it did, in two critical ways.

Adjustable-Rate Mortgages

First, the industry introduced the *adjustable-rate mortgage*, or ARM. In an ARM, which we will discuss at length in Chapter 9, the interest rate paid on the mortgage adjusts periodically in line with some general index of interest rates. Most of the interest rate risk is shifted from the lender to the borrower. If interest rates rise, the lender is largely protected.

In a relatively few years, ARMs have come to represent a substantial part of the new mortgages issued— a remarkably quick change in an old industry. And with the ARM has come a dazzling range of variations tailored to meet the needs of the lender (and occasionally the borrower)—which we like to call *designer mortgages*, and which will be discussed in Chapter 10.

The Secondary Market

At the same time, it became apparent that the traditional mortgage lending institutions—savings and loans, commercial banks, savings banks—didn't have the lending capacity or risk-taking capacity to satisfy the needs of a growing mortgage market. And so there began a great expansion of the *secondary market*—the market in which mortgages are sold by the original lender to other investors, bringing new capital into the market and freeing the lender's funds so that the lender once again has the capacity to originate new mortgages.

Financial institutions developed new ways of putting together packages of mortgages and selling them to investors. Ways were found of assuring these investors that their investments were safe. With this assurance, the secondary market grew at a remarkable rate.

Fannie, Ginnie, and Freddie

Three government agencies—nicknamed Fannie Mae, Ginnie Mae, and Freddie Mac—have played an important part in this growth. While you, as a home buyer or home owner, don't really have to be concerned about the secondary market, you will hear the names of these agencies so often that we will tell you briefly who they are.

The Federal National Mortgage Association, known

as Fannie Mae (FNMA), was chartered by the government in 1938. It raises capital by borrowing from the public, and uses the money to buy mortgages from mortgage lenders, giving the lenders cash to begin the cycle over again. In 1970 Fannie Mae became a private business, owned by participating lenders and the public, but it retains some of the privileges of a governmental agency.

The Government National Mortgage Association (Ginnie Mae) (GNMA) is actually part of the Department of Housing and Urban Development (HUD). It buys certain mortgages, packages them into pools, and sells participations in these pools to investors, who receive monthly payments representing both principal and interest. These participations, termed *pass-through certificates*, carry the "full faith and credit" of the U.S. government—the best of all guarantees—and have become immensely popular with investors as a result.

The Federal Home Loan Mortgage Corporation (Freddie Mac), the third and last of the trio, is part of the Federal Home Loan Bank Board, which oversees savings and loan associations. It buys certain mortgages, raising capital by selling mortgage-backed bonds to the public.

As we said above, this secondary market doesn't directly concern you. Or perhaps it does. The financial system has been brilliantly creative in developing new institutions to meet new financial needs. Because of Fannie Mae, Ginnie Mae, and Freddie Mac, your local bank, savings and loan, and mortgage service agency are all far more able than they would otherwise be to give you a sizeable mortgage on reasonable terms—which is what this book is all about.

5

WHERE DO YOU GET A MORTGAGE LOAN?

There are many sources of mortgage money. If possible, you should check into all of them.

Who Will Help You—Your Broker

The *real estate broker* who sold you the house will probably be very helpful in directing you to willing mortgage lenders. Contact the people he or she suggests, and then do some shopping for yourself. Shopping may be time consuming, but when you think of the total cost of your house, and add up the interest to be paid over the life of the loan, you will see that the time is definitely well spent.

You should be aware that the real estate person is possibly getting a small fee (perhaps $150) from the mortgage lender for referring you to them. This kickback should not worry you unduly, because the financial institution pays the fee, not you. It is, however, another reason for you to shop around. A bank which is not paying a fee may give you a better deal.

Builder Financing

The *builder* of a new house will probably have mortgage money lined up for qualified buyers. The rates will often be attractive, and you may well end up using this arrangement, but you should shop around anyway. You can never tell when you might be able to find a better deal for yourself.

Sometimes the builder may be willing to give you

an extra break on mortgage money, especially if he or she is in financial trouble or is in need of making that first critical sale.

Attorney Assistance

Your *attorney* could prove to be a good source of mortgage information. The added assistance a good real estate lawyer can give you in this area is one of the many reasons to choose your lawyer carefully.

You should ask your friends or colleagues to recommend an attorney with whom they have had successful real estate experience, and you should take the time to interview him or her. If you cannot get a recommendation from someone you know, call the local bar association for a list of attorneys specializing in real estate, and contact several on the list.

Don't be shy about interviewing an attorney. Ask questions, especially about his or her prior experience in real estate and, if you are buying a co-op or condominium, about specific experience in those areas. Ask about contacts with mortgage lenders. And, most importantly, ask about fees. Know what you are getting into before you hire an attorney. Remember that the right lawyer can save you money, grief and heartache by clearing up problems before they become insoluble.

Who Has Money to Lend?—Seller Financing

As for the actual potential lenders of money, if you have bought an older house, begin with the person who sells you your house. Don't hesitate to ask if he or she will take back all or part of the sale price in the form of a mortgage. Seller financing is especially popular with older sellers, who look forward to the steady income such an arrangement can provide.

Banking Institutions

Banks are, of course, the most obvious source of money. There are several types of banking institutions involved in the mortgage business. Commercial banks are important mortgage lenders. Savings and loan associations, called building and loan associations in some areas, traditionally put most of their depositors' money into mortgages and are a mainstay of the housing industry. Mutual savings banks (located mostly in New England and similar to savings and loans) are also sources.

Credit Unions

Credit unions are usually the cheapest source of mortgage money. If you belong to a credit union, do not hesitate to inquire there first. It could save you a lot of shoe leather.

Mortgage Service Companies

Mortgage service companies, also known as mortgage brokers or mortgage bankers, are service companies which deal exclusively in the mortgage lending business. They are state licensed and regulated and, because they specialize, they frequently offer loans at discount rates.

Mortgage service companies operate in two ways. They may originate the mortgage loans, packaging groups of them for resale to governmental agencies (or to other entities which buy mortgages, such as pension funds, life insurance companies and mutual funds). Or they may act as representatives of banks, savings and loans, credit unions and other lenders in processing mortgages.

Note that while these companies are loan *originators*, they are not long-term lenders themselves. They only act as servicing agents over the long term, as processing agents for the actual long-term lender.

A bank may buy mortgage loans from a mortgage service company in order to spread the bank's risk over many loans in various parts of the country. And the bank may be glad to have the service company process the loans. A mortgage service company typically charges between ¼ and ½ of 1% of the loan as an annual servicing fee for collecting the interest and principal each month for the mortgage holder. In addition, they may receive a one-time origination fee of 1% to 1½% of the loan. They also act as an escrow agent, collecting the insurance premiums and real estate taxes.

A mortgage service company will quite frequently offer you the best deal in town. Mortgages are their business, and they have to remain competitive in order to stay ahead. So check several mortgage bankers before you make your final selection. In addition, the mortgage companies frequently work with the new computerized mortgage networks (see Chapter 6) and may be able to give you a mortgage commitment in as little as 30 minutes if you meet certain requirements, such as a down payment of 30%.

Family Assistance

Family members or friends should never be overlooked when making as big an investment as buying a house. Parents and rich relatives might just be willing to help you out. If such an arrangement is possible, first make sure that it won't lead to strained family relations. Then, draw up a simple loan agreement (or have your lawyer draw it up), sign it, and make sure you stick to it.

6

SHOP, SHOP, SHOP

With so many potential lenders to choose from and so many different types of mortgages available, the first rule to remember is a simple one—shop, shop, shop.

Every bank, every savings and loan and every other mortgage institution has its own set of rules and criteria. The variety of mortgages available to you today is mind-boggling. Don't panic—simply take time to shop around until you are sure that the deal you select is the best one for you.

The second thing to remember is that, while a deal may *sound* great, you have to take the time to check the actual numbers before you sign on the dotted line. Plan to give your calculator (or someone's calculator) a good workout.

Don't forget that mortgage interest payments are tax-deductible, while principal repayments are not. You have to calculate your tax savings under each arrangement, and include those in the comparison. It is only by doing the mathematics, or having them done for you, that you can understand how much you will actually pay and which deal works out best.

Computer Mortgage Networks

There are two new businesses that have arisen to make your shopping easier and to help you find your way through the variety of the mortgage market. The first are the computerized mortgage origination networks. These are usually located in real estate offices. Your application and relevant financial data are fed

11

into the computer terminal, and a mortgage commitment can sometimes be received in as little as 30 minutes.

Mortgage Consultants

The second new business is the mortgage consulting business. Mortgage consultants counsel the buyer and process his or her application for lenders who subscribe to the service. Here the objective is help, not speed; the mortgage decision is usually not any quicker than if you had applied yourself.

Mortgage networks and consultants work in the same way as do travel agents. They do not charge a fee to the borrower who uses their service. Rather they are paid by the lender for performing services that the lender can now avoid. The borrower pays the standard fees that would have to be paid to a mortgage lender, including appraisal of the property (usually about $150 to $200) and a credit check (about $25 or $30).

As of the writing of this book, these avenues of mortgage hunting have not been time tested. We suggest that if you decide to use the services of a mortgage consultant or mortgage network, you compare the mortgage offered you against other lenders by doing some legwork of your own. Be careful that the interest rates offered to you by these new businesses do not include an added amount to pay for their services. In other words—shop, shop, shop.

Mortgage Reporting Services

Finally, you should check to see if mortgage data weeklies or mortgage reporting services, which have been popping up all over the country, are available in your area. The best of these are definitely worth the expense (subscription costs begin at about $25). These publications tell you where the mortgage money is, the interest rates being offered, and the qualifications you must meet for each listed lender. They give you the details on additional charges, including points, origination fees, application fees and maximum amount of the loan. They will save you much legwork that you would otherwise spend in checking interest rates and finding out whether or not you qualify for the cheapest loans.

7

TYPES OF MORTGAGES: AN OVERVIEW

Mortgages can be classified in several ways. One important distinction is between conventional mortgages and federally sponsored mortgages.

Conventional Mortgages

A conventional mortgage is any type of mortgage loan that is not insured by an agency of the federal government. Conventional mortgages can be either the standard fixed-rate loan or the new adjustable-rate variety.

The majority of people obtain a conventional mortgage loan. Remember that it is not the actual terms of the loan, the number of years it will run, or the interest rate that makes it conventional—it is simply that it does not have government insurance. As a result, the prevailing interest rate on conventional mortgages will generally be higher than on government-insured mortgages.

The fact that your conventional mortgage may be resold to Fannie Mae, Freddie Mac or Ginnie Mae (see Chapter 4) does not change the basic character of your loan. If it is made conventionally, it remains a conventional mortgage throughout its life.

Down Payment

Conventional loans usually require a larger down payment than federally backed ones. If you can't afford the large (20% or so) down payment, but are considered a good risk by your lender, you may have to purchase a type of mortgage insurance. Mortgage insurance will be discussed in Chapter 13.

Assumability

Conventional mortgages are often not assumable by future buyers of your house. In fact, many states have laws which prevent conventional mortgages from being assumable.

Federally Backed Mortgages

We now turn to federally backed mortgages. These include loans that are secured by the Federal Housing Authority (FHA), the Veterans Administration (VA), and the Farmers Home Administration (FmHA).

FHA

The purpose of the Federal Housing Authority (FHA) of the U.S. Department of Housing and Urban Development (HUD) is to encourage home ownership by those who, without the assistance of the federal government, would not be able to afford to buy their own home.

The Federal Housing Authority (FHA) does not actually have mortgage money to lend, but it does have loan insurance programs that can help you get 30-year mortgage loans with a small down payment. These programs insure your mortgage against default. In order to determine the down payment, you add the sale price plus the closing costs or the appraisal value plus the closing costs, and find which sum is lower. Recently, if that sum is less than $50,000, your down payment will be 3%. If, however, the sum is $50,000 or more, your down payment will be 3% on the first $25,000 and 5% on all amounts over that.

There are no specific economic qualifications for borrowers to receive FHA insurance. But the property, which may be urban or rural, new or existing, must meet the HUD Minimum Property Standards. And there is a maximum dollar limit above which the FHA will not insure. The basic limit on a single-family home

15

is about $67,500. But this maximum varies according to locale, so we suggest you contact HUD to see if your house qualifies.

In addition, the FHA has several specialized programs to assist displaced persons or those who have been the victims of disasters. Your local HUD field office will supply you with a complete program list.

Mortgage companies often specialize in processing FHA mortgages, and they will usually process the paperwork for you. Remember that it is up to the seller of the house to decide whether or not to allow an FHA mortgage. A seller might be hesitant about an FHA mortgage because it could cost him or her extra money in order to meet the inspection and minimum standard requirements.

In addition to the economic advantage of FHA assistance, all FHA loans are assumable. This means that if you decide to sell your house, the buyer will be able to assume your old mortgage at your interest rate. If your interest rate is lower than the going rate at the time of resale, this feature will add extra value to your house.

The FHA also publishes many informative booklets on various housing subjects, available either free or at a minimal cost from your local FHA office or the Government Printing Office.

Veterans Administration

The Veterans Administration guarantees that eligible veterans will be able to get mortgages with *no money down*. If the veteran defaults, the VA will pay off the mortgage loan. Like FHA loans, VA loans are assumable. However, the amount of available money is limited, and the requirements for getting a VA loan (maximum income and savings, etc.) have become stricter.

If you are a veteran, you should certainly check your eligibility with the VA. Or take your discharge papers to your mortgage lender and file a request for a Certificate of Eligibility. In some areas, mortgage lenders will require the veteran to obtain the certificate directly from the VA. Once a Certificate of Eligi-

16

bility has been obtained, the mortgage will be issued. The government establishes the VA rate, and while it is usually lower than the normal rate, mortgage lenders are pleased to issue VA mortgages because they are insured by Uncle Sam.

FmHA

Farmers Home Administration (FmHA) loans are available to farmers and to nonfarmers who live within specified rural areas and who meet certain low-income requirements. The FmHA is part of the U.S. Department of Agriculture, and, if you think that you might meet the requirements, you should definitely take the time to contact them.

State Programs

Some states offer special low interest, low down payment deals for qualified low-income buyers. Others distribute mortgage money through a lottery system, with qualified buyers receiving money by the luck of the draw. You should contact your local and state governments to see if you qualify and how to apply.

8

FIXED-RATE MORTGAGES

A fixed-rate mortgage is the standard, old reliable mortgage that your parents had and that, until recently, was the only kind of mortgage available.

In a fixed-rate mortgage, the interest rate is determined at the time the loan is arranged and that rate remains constant through the life of the loan. You always know how much your monthly payments will be, because they never vary from the first to the last installment.

The consistency and security of knowing exactly how much your payments will be is certainly an advantage of the fixed-rate loan. Unlike the case with adjustable-rate mortgages (Chapter 9), your payments will not be subject to the fluctuations and vagaries of the interest rate market.

Should you take out a shorter-term or a longer-term mortgage? The difference in monthly payments may be less than you would have assumed. A few examples of the monthly payments on a 15-year or 30-year mortgage at a fixed rate of 10% are shown in the following table.

Amount of Loan	Rate	Payment @15 years	Payment @30 years
$40,000	10%	$430	$351
70,000	10%	752	614
100,000	10%	1,075	878

On the following page is an expanded table showing monthly payments over a wide range of possible

Payments on a 30-Year and a 15-Year Mortgage
(on a $100,000 mortgage)

Term of Mortgage	7%	8%	9%	10%	11%	13%	15%
30-Year Mortgage							
Monthly Payment (a)......	$665.31	$733.77	$804.62	$877.57	$952.32	$1106.19	$1264.44
Total Interest Paid (b)	139,512	164,157	189,663	215,925	242,835	298,228	355,198
15-Year Mortgage							
Monthly Payment (a)......	$898.83	$955.66	$1014.26	$1074.60	$1136.59	$1265.24	$1399.58
Total Interest Paid (b)	61,789	72,019	82,567	93,428	104,586	127,743	151,924

(a) On fixed-rate mortgage, including principal repayment and interest.
(b) Total interest paid over life of mortgage, not including $100,000 principal repayment.

fixed-interest rates. The payments are shown for a $100,000 mortgage. To calculate the payments on a $40,000 mortgage, simply multiply the figures in the table by 0.4; for a $70,000 mortgage by 0.7; and so forth.

Lenders are less likely to give fixed-rate loans during periods of inflation and sharp interest rate fluctuations, because they fear that interest rates may then soar, and they will have lent out their money at too low a rate. Because of the desire of the lending institutions for protection, the interest rate on a fixed-rate mortgage tends to be higher than the initial interest rate on an adjustable mortgage.

Assumability

Most fixed-rate instruments are not assumable, except those backed by the FHA or VA.

Locking in an Interest Rate

Usually the lender will not lock in a rate of interest until the loan is processed and approved, a procedure that could take 60 days or so. If interest rates are particularly favorable at the time you apply, you might try to find a lender who will commit to the current rate when you apply. You can sometimes pay a lender to lock in the interest rate. This may look like an expensive way of proceeding, as the lender often charges ½ of 1% of the loan value to lock in a rate. But if rates do go up while you are waiting, this one-time charge of a few hundred dollars could save you thousands of dollars over the life of the loan. And many mortgage lenders will apply the lock-in charge against *points* owed at settlement. (See Chapter 14.)

9

ADJUSTABLE-RATE MORTGAGES (ARMs)

In Chapter 4, we discussed the problems that mortgage lenders had as interest rates went wild in the late 1970s and early 1980s. Their response was the development of the adjustable-rate mortgage (ARM) and of a whole range of variations which we call *designer mortgages*.

If you have decided on a fixed-rate mortgage, the many varieties of adjustable-rate and designer mortgages may not be relevant to you. But as they represent interesting and sometimes creative opportunities, you should be aware of what they are, remembering that lenders may offer only certain of these at any given time, depending on the local mortgage market.

There are many types of designer mortgages, to suit many needs. You will find that the needs that are answered are mostly those of the lender, rather than of the borrower. But with so many varieties of loans to choose from, and more types of lenders competing, the borrower has advantages, too.

Truth in Lending

The federal Truth in Lending Act requires mortgage lenders to disclose the "annual percentage rate" (APR) charged to the borrower. The APR must be the effective rate—that is, the *real* rate charged—taking into account all financing charges, including insurance premiums, origination fees and "points." (See Chapter 14.) However, you should note that in the case of an ARM, the stated APR assumes that the index will remain the same for the entire length of the loan—that is, it does not show how the payments will change as the interest rate fluctuates.

ARM

The basic adjustable-rate mortgage (ARM) is usually called an adjustable mortgage loan (AML) at federal savings and loan associations, and is also referred to as a variable-rate mortgage or a renegotiable-rate mortgage. For convenience and brevity, we will refer to all of these as ARMs, as they are alike in almost every respect.

An ARM is a mortgage where an initial interest rate is set at the time the loan is contracted, but the interest rate is adjusted at fixed intervals during the life of the loan according to a specific index. This index is some accepted indicator of interest rates—for example, the current 90-day Treasury bill rate (the interest rate the U.S. Treasury pays on its shortest-term borrowings), or the rate on longer-term Treasury borrowings. So, the interest rate you pay on your mortgage loan changes periodically based on fluctuations in the general level of interest rates.

Initial interest rates on ARMs tend to be lower than those on fixed-rate instruments because in an ARM, you assume much of the risk of interest rate fluctuations, and the lender needs less protection against a possible future rise in interest rates—the lender's protection is built into the ARM.

Interest Rate Fluctuations

Obviously, if you think that interest rates are going up, you will prefer to get a fixed-rate loan and lock in the lower rate. If, however, you think that interest rates are going down, an ARM would be preferable. How do you know what is going to happen to interest rates in the future? You probably don't. Interest rate fluctuations make up one of the greatest guessing games of the financial world, and the "experts" are quite often wrong in their predictions. Over the long run, interest rates tend to rise when inflation is high, and to fall when inflation cools; but other factors also come into play, and the shorter-term fluctuations can be unpredictable.

What Does Interest Actually Cost?

You may be amazed to find out how much interest you actually pay on a mortgage loan. Consider that if you have a 10%, 30-year mortgage loan of $40,000, you will end up paying $86,367 in interest, or a total of $126,367! If you have the same terms, but a $70,000 loan, you will pay $151,148 in interest, and with a $100,000 loan you will pay $215,925!

If you were to shorten the term of the loan to 15 years, your monthly payments would be higher but you would sharply reduce the total amount of interest you pay. This doesn't necessarily mean that a shorter-term loan is better; it depends on your individual needs.

On the following page is a table that shows how much interest you will actually pay on different size mortgages at varying interest rates. Note that the numbers in this table *do not* include the principal amount of your mortgage, in this case, $40,000, $70,000, or $100,000.

Understand the Choices

How do you choose which mortgage to take? There's no easy shortcut—you have to shop around and see what's available. Then you do all the mathematics regarding the loan (or have a friend's computer do the math for you). Then, based on your financial status and expectations, you pick the deal that you think is best for you. The only way to decide is to understand the choices.

Check the Long-term Effect

It goes without saying that you must look not only at the first few years of the loan, but at the long-term effect of the adjustable rate. Figure out what your payments *could* be as time goes on, rather than focusing on the great deal you have initially.

Total Interest Payments on a Mortgage

Mortgage Term $ Amount	Interest Rate								
	7%	8%	9%	10%	11%	12%	13%	14%	15%
15 Years									
$ 40,000	$ 24,716	$ 28,808	$ 33,026	$ 37,371	$ 41,833	$ 46,411	$ 51,096	$ 55,885	$ 60,769
70,000	43,252	50,413	57,796	65,400	73,210	81,220	89,419	97,798	106,348
100,000	61,789	72,019	82,567	93,428	104,586	116,029	127,743	139,713	151,924
30 Years									
$ 40,000	$ 55,804	$ 65,662	$ 75,862	$ 86,367	$ 97,131	$108,118	$119,289	$130,622	$142,077
70,000	97,656	114,909	132,763	151,148	169,983	189,207	208,759	228,588	248,640
100,000	139,512	164,157	189,663	215,925	242,835	270,300	298,228	326,553	355,198

The Index

The index an adjustable loan uses is of the utmost importance. You must find out which index is being used and how frequently your rate can be adjusted. The longer the period between reviews, the more stability you will have in the amount you have to pay. Obviously, unless you are confident that interest rates are going down, you should try for as few recalculations of your rate as possible.

As noted above, many ARMs use the interest rate on short-term U.S. Treasury securities as the index. Others use the Federal Home Loan Bank Board national average mortgage contract percent. Another possible index which offers an advantage to borrowers is the rate on three-year U.S. Treasury securities—this rate is more stable and less volatile than that on short-term Treasury bills.

ARM contracts may call for reevaluation every 6 months or every 1, 3, or 5 years. The longer the time between recalculations, the better for the borrower.

Shifting Index

It's important to see if your lender can change the index during the course of the loan. This is a common trick to help the lender get the highest interest rate possible. By all means try to see that only one index is used for the life of the loan, rather than giving the lender the ability to change the rules at your expense.

Margin

In addition to understanding the index used and the frequency of recalculation, it is also important to understand the *margin* that will be added to the index to arrive at the interest rate you actually pay. This margin will vary depending on the index used and your particular loan arrangement. The margin may, for example, be 2½% or 3% if you are using a Treasury bill index, but it should be small or zero if you are using a national mortgage index.

Let's look at this example: your initial interest rate is 9%. In 3 years, it's time for a rate adjustment, and Treasury bills (your index) are now paying 8%. Sounds great? Not really. Your lender has built in a margin of 2½%, so your rate will go up to 10½% (8% plus 2½%). And your monthly payments will be adjusted upward accordingly.

Caps

If interest rates go up considerably, your ARM can turn out to be very expensive. You can protect yourself against unlimited skyrocketing of payments by making sure that your mortgage includes a *cap* provision.

There are two kinds of caps—a life cap and an adjustment cap. And the cap can be on the interest rate or on the dollar amount you can pay each month.

A life cap puts a maximum on the amount that your interest rate or monthly payments can be raised over the entire life of the loan.

An adjustment cap puts a maximum on the amount of each individual adjustment. Look for an ARM that has both kinds of caps. A favorable mortgage, for example, might be one that limits interest rate increases to a maximum of ½% at each adjustment period and a total of 5% over the life of the loan.

Just as there may be an upper cap on interest rates, there may be a minimum cap, too. Check to see how far down your payments will be allowed to drop if interest rates tumble.

Beware of Cut-rate Bargains

Many lenders give fantastic cut-rate deals for the first year or so of an ARM. These can be just that—fantastic deals. Or they can be traps. Some lenders may offer you 8% or even 6% or less as the first year interest rate.

As unbeatable as that sounds, check the fine print. In fact, the more unbeatable it sounds, the more carefully you should check the terms. Very often you pay dearly later on for a cut-rate beginning.

Negative Amortization

One of the perils of a bargain beginning is that you may later run into *negative amortization.*

Amortization is the process by which you gradually pay off the principal amount of your mortgage loan. *Negative amortization* is what happens when the process goes into reverse. If your monthly payments at the beginning are capped so low that you are not even paying the effective interest charges on the mortgage, the lender may have the right to add the difference to the *principal* of your loan. So, while you are making bargain monthly payments, you are actually accumulating more and more debt.

Negative amortization is so insidious that many lenders have given up the practice, and it is no longer common. But if you are taking out an ARM with a low initial rate, be sure to find out if the payment schedule does, in fact, involve negative amortization.

Here's how negative amortization can work. It's usual for the initial interest rate not to be tied to the index, which is how cut-rate deals are possible. Let's say that you pay a 5% initial interest rate for the first year. And let's say that for the first year and for all subsequent years the index calls for an interest rate of 9¾%. (A non-fluctuating index rate is highly unlikely, but we use it here to simplify our example.) Let's also assume a 7½% cap on payments for years 1 through 4—when your payments are adjusted in these years, the maximum increase can only be 7½% at each step, no matter how high the index is. The following table shows how this works out. For the first four years, while you are enjoying your bargain payments, your loan is actually *increasing* in size. Later on, of course, you will have to pay more to make up for this. Not a good situation, and not a nice surprise for unwary borrowers.

Amount of Loan	Index Percent	Number of Yrs.	Year Number	Monthly Payments	Loan Balance
$70,000	5%	1	1	$375.78	$72,422
	9¾%	29	2	403.96	74,737
			3	434.26	76,908
			4	466.83	78,829
			5–30	696.80	–

Caps and Negative Amortization

You should note that many mortgage loans have a total cap on negative amortization. This cap is often 125% of the original mortgage balance, so that if your original loan is $100,000, the lender will only negatively amortize up to a loan balance of $125,000. Beware! If that happens, you will sometimes be required to come up with a lump-sum payment or some refinancing arrangement to keep the loan balance from rising above the limit.

Negative amortization is definitely something to be concerned about in an ARM. However, if *your mortgage has a cap on interest rates, rather than on payments, there will be no negative amortization.*

Let's take an example similar to the above, but assume now that the only cap is one limiting the increase in your interest rate to ½% each year. Let's assume that you start at 7%. Your rate would increase like this:

Year	Rate
1	7 %
2	7½%
3	8 %
4	8½%
5	9 %
6	9½%
7	9¾%
8	9¾%

Your monthly payments would rise each year in years 2 through 7, but there would be no "deficit" in your payments, and the principal amount of your loan would gradually be reduced. It's a better arrangement.

Prepayment Penalty

Always check to see if you can refinance your mortgage loan (or pay it off early) without a penalty. This penalty, often called a prepayment penalty, assesses a monetary fine (sometimes as much as 6 months' interest) on a borrower who wants to pay off the mortgage in advance of the regular time. We will discuss refinancing in Chapter 19.

Read First

How do you avoid these problems? Read the entire loan contract carefully, and seek expert assistance if you need an interpretation (which may well be the case). And, if you think that negative amortization may be a problem with a specific loan, shop around until you find one without the problem.

Get the Details

You should get from your lender a statement of exactly how your loan will work, in detail. If elements of the loan are not explained in clear terms in the statement you receive, *demand clarification before you pay any fees and before you sign.* All nationally chartered banks must give you information on how your ARM will work if interest rates go up by 2% over 5 years. They also must tell you which index is being used. We repeat: Don't sign for an ARM until you (a) know just what the rules are and (b) understand fully how they may actually work out.

Conclusion

There are four principles to remember when dealing with ARMs:

1. The lower the maximum and minimum caps are, the better.
2. A cap on the interest rate (rather than on payments) will avoid the problem of negative amortization.
3. The less frequently the interest rates are adjusted, the better.
4. The more stable the chosen index is, and the less subject to wild fluctuations, the better.

10

MORE DESIGNER STYLES

We have discussed some of the major choices that you may have to make in adjustable rate mortgages (ARMs). But there are all sorts of other choices, variations, and new types of mortgage loans that you should know about. We will discuss some of these choices and designer styles alphabetically.

Assumption of Existing Mortgage

When you buy an older house, you should always check with the seller to see if his or her mortgage loan is assumable. Some loans, notably those that are backed by federal agencies like the FHA or VA, can be assumed by the buyer. Assumability means that the new owner can take over the existing mortgage loan and its interest rate.

This can be an excellent arrangement for both the buyer and the seller. For the buyer, a mortgage loan that is several years old will probably be at a lower, more favorable, interest rate. For the seller, assumability helps the buyer get the required financing to consummate the purchase.

The buyer will have to pay the seller in cash (unless otherwise agreed) the amount by which the agreed-upon sale price exceeds the current principal amount of the mortgage.

For example, let's say that you have agreed to buy a house with an assumable mortgage for a price of $70,000. The original mortgage was for $50,000, at a fixed rate of 8%, and for 25 years. The mortgage is now 10 years old. With this type of fixed-rate mortgage loan, the monthly payments are $385.91 per month. As you know by now, mortgage payments in the first few years go mainly to pay interest due on the loan, and very little is applied against the principal. So, the principal balance remaining on this mortgage loan has been reduced only to $40,380. Since you owe the seller $70,000 in total, you will have to pay the balance of $29,620 in cash.

This cash outlay ($29,620) is similar to down payment money. In order to keep the amount of cash to be put up as small as possible, you should look for a not-so-old VA or FHA loan, similar to the one in our example. You will usually have to put up more cash than if you were taking out a new mortgage, but your monthly payments may be dramatically lower. In this example, if you had taken out a new 25-year, fixed-rate mortgage for $56,000 at 10½%, your monthly payments would be $528.76, instead of $385.91. And remember that you would be paying off this new mortgage for 25 years, while the old 8% mortgage has only another 15 years to go.

If you don't have the cash needed to bridge the gap between the assumed mortgage and the purchase price, you can probably get a second mortgage either from the seller or a lending institution. The rate on the second mortgage will be higher than the going rate on a first mortgage because the lender's claim on your property comes after the claim of the first mortgage holder. In the example above, you might pay a high rate on a second mortgage of $10,000 to $20,000, but, because you are paying a low rate on the larger first mortgage, you are still far better off than if you were to refinance the whole purchase at current rates.

Remember that most conventional loans are not assumable. Some states have even passed laws at the urging of the mortgage industry to prevent assumability.

Balloon Mortgage

With a balloon mortgage, the loan behaves initially like a regular fixed-rate mortgage. You make payments at the same rate as if the debt were scheduled to last, say, 30 years. However, you only make these payments for a specific shorter number of years, often 3 or 5, or perhaps 10. At the conclusion of that time, the entire remaining principal amount becomes due.

Here is an example: Let's assume you have a 30-year mortgage for $40,000 at 10% with a 3-year balloon. Each month for 35 months (just short of the 3 years) you will pay $351.03. In the 36th month, however, you will have to pay the mortgage lender $39,611, which is the balance due on your mortgage loan. The payments you made in the first years of your mortgage went largely, as usual, to pay the interest, with little being applied to repay principal. This is why your balance remains so high.

Assuming the same facts, but with a 5-year balloon, your monthly payments would again be $351.03, and your loan payoff at the end of the 5th year would be $38,979. With a 10-year balloon, the balance due at the end of the 10th year would be $36,727. The following table gives examples with larger principal amounts.

Examples of Balloon Mortgages

Amount of Loan	Rate	Balloon Payment Due at the End of Year Number		
		3	5	10
$ 70,000	10%	$69,320	$68,210	$64,270
100,000	10%	99,030	97,450	91,820

In certain special situations, when the lenders in an area are limiting their commitments and afraid of higher interest rates, you may have no choice but to take a balloon mortgage. The problem with a balloon mortgage is that you must refinance at balloon time, with all the added expense and grief that may entail. Also, with a balloon that comes due rather quickly, you will have paid a great deal of interest but very little principal at the time you must refinance. Because of this, you will have little equity (ownership) in the house, and little bargaining power with your new lender.

Blended Mortgage

The blended mortgage is a secretive ruse which we mention only to tell you not to try it. In this scheme, the existing mortgage is not assumable, but the buyer and the seller decide to try to fool the mortgage lender so that the buyer can assume the mortgage anyway. Don't do it. Mortgage lenders have many ways of finding out if you are cheating (such as checking the name on the home insurance policy).

The penalty for discovery of this scam can be substantial. If there is a due-on-sale clause in the mortgage, and the lender finds out that you are cheating, the lender can call the entire outstanding amount due immediately. This could force you into disastrous negotiations with the lender, with all the cards stacked against you. And if you can't immediately get a new loan, the property will be sold at a sacrifice sale.

Buy-downs

There are two types of buy-downs—permanent and temporary. In a permanent buy-down, the builder of a new house or the seller of an older one will pay the mortgage lender a lump sum in order for the buyer to get a lower interest rate. Many new house builders use this as an inducement to buy; it is a way of giving you a concession without dropping the stated price. But make sure that the purchase price of the house is not inflated to make up for the amount the builder or seller pays for the buy-down.

A temporary buy-down is similar, except that the interest rate is lowered only for a limited number of years through the payment of a lump sum by the builder or seller. A typical builder buy-down is to pay for 3 interest points (3%) in the first year of the mortgage, 2% in the second, and 1% in the third. Because the monthly mortgage payments have been reduced, the buyer's income requirements for obtaining the mortgage will also be reduced. The buyer must be sure that after the buy-down runs out, he or she can then afford the regular monthly payments.

Let's say that you have obtained a mortgage with an interest rate of 10%. In our above example, the builder will pay to the lender enough cash to cover the difference between 10% and 7% for the first year, 10% and 8% for the second year and 10% and 9% for the third year. You will pay only the lower rates (7%, 8%, and 9%). A very good deal.

Contract Sale

A contract sale, also known as a contract for deed, is another scheme to get around a nonassumable mortgage with a due-on-sale clause. Because this procedure offers little or no protection to the buyer, we do not recommend it.

In a contract sale, the buyer makes the monthly mortgage and related payments to the seller, who submits them as if he or she were still living in the property. Title doesn't actually pass to the buyer until the contract period is over—that is, when the mortgage loan is fully paid off. With 30-year loans commonplace, the contract could have a very long time to run before title, or legal ownership of the property, passes to the buyer.

The buyer still has to give the seller, in advance, a cash amount equal to the equity and profit. And, worst of all, the buyer really has no assurance that the seller is actually using his or her money to pay off the mortgage and taxes. An unscrupulous seller could pocket the money and allow liens to accumulate against the property.

Contract sales are good schemes to avoid. But if you decide to try this route, make sure you see a real estate lawyer for assistance in preparing the contract documents.

Elastic Mortgage

An elastic mortgage is one of the most creative mortgages we've seen. It combines the stability of fixed monthly payments with the flexibility of an ARM.

How does it do this? An elastic mortgage begins as a 15-year mortgage, with monthly payments fixed, permanently and absolutely, as of the date the mortgage is granted. If you pay $850 the first month, you will pay $850 each and every month thereafter. But, unlike a fixed-rate loan, the interest rate can change, according to the index used (usually long-term Treasury bonds).

This change in interest rate is not reflected in the amount of your monthly payments; as stated above, they remain constant. It is reflected in the *number of payments* you make. If the index rate declines, it is possible that your monthly payments will end before the end of the originally contracted 15 years. But if the interest rate index rises, you may have to make more payments, stretching beyond the original 15 years. So it is the term which varies, not the amount of your monthly payment.

Interest rates on elastic mortgages are usually pegged initially about 2% below rates on a regular fixed-rate instrument, since here, as with a regular ARM, you are taking a large part of the interest rate risk away from the lender. These loans are generally assumable (depending on the state), and carry a lifetime rate cap and no prepayment penalty.

Fixed-Rate Mortgage with a Call Option

This mortgage operates like an ordinary fixed-rate instrument, except that it has an additional provision similar to a balloon mortgage. Upon the occurrence of a pre-determined condition, the lender can "call" the loan. This means that the lender can demand immediate payment of the entire outstanding sum of the loan.

The buyer must then pay off and refinance. This could come at a time when interest rates are high. The uncertainty of a call option makes it one of our least favorite choices.

Flexible Loan Insurance Program

These mortgages are written in two stages. During the first stage, only interest is paid. During the next stage, the debt is repaid. But since the debt repayment is done in a shorter period of time, the monthly payments are larger than for an ordinary fixed-rate mortgage.

Graduated Payment Mortgage (GPM)

The Graduated Payment Mortgage (GPM) became popular during the high-interest rate period of the early 1980s. GPMs can be either fixed-rate or adjustable-rate. The GPM was based on the theory that many people, especially young people just getting started, can't afford large monthly payments, but will be able to do so in the future.

The GPM theory is a good one, if you fit into the category described. You will have smaller payments at the beginning of the loan, and the payments will rise on a fixed schedule over a predetermined number of years (usually 5, but sometimes 10).

One big advantage of the GPM is that it is often easier to qualify for, since the early payments will be smaller relative to your income. One big problem is that there may not be a cap on the maximum interest that can be charged in the future, and the early advantage may prove very costly later. This is especially true when you add the possible effects of negative amortization (see Chapter 9) into the arithmetic.

As an example of a graduated payment mortgage during a relatively high-interest rate period, let's assume that you get a $40,000 GPM at 12½% for 30 years. The payments that you make for the first years (in our example, 5 years) will not reflect the 12½% interest rate. Rather, they will be precalculated based on an escalating scale that allows you to begin to amortize your loan (that is, to begin to pay off the principal) in the 6th year. The payments escalate based on a fixed percentage, in our example (and commonly) 7½% per year. This is how it works:

With a $40,000 mortgage, at 12½%, for 30 years, you will pay $329.43 per month for the first 12 months. Because the amount you pay does not reflect the *real* interest rate of 12½%, there is a pre-set negative amortization built into the calculations. But in this case the negative amortization is intentional, you know exactly what the negative amortization is and how it will accumulate, and there are no surprises. The negative amortization makes your loan balance

$41,108.95 at the end of the first year. The first table below illustrates the changing monthly payments and loan balance over the first 5 years of the loan in this example. In the succeeding table, the same information is given, but this time for a $70,000, 12½%, 30-year mortgage loan.

You will note that the loan balance actually goes up in years 1 through 5 because of the negative amortization. If this had been a $40,000 fixed-rate mortgage at 12½% for 30 years, your monthly payments would have been a constant $426.90. So the monthly payments in our example end up being $46.04 more each month for the privilege of paying less in the beginning. This can be a useful deal, if you are sure you will be able to afford the final payments.

$40,000 GPM at 12½% for 30 years

Amount of Loan	Interest Rate	Number Of Years	Year No.	Monthly Payment	Loan Balance
$40,000	12½%	30	1	$329.43	$41,108.95
			2	354.14	42,050.63
			3	380.70	42,779.38
			4	409.25	43,241.69
			5	439.94	43,375.08
			6–30	472.94	0.00

$70,000 GPM at 12½% for 30 years

Amount of Loan	Interest Rate	Number of Years	Year No.	Monthly Payment	Loan Balance
$70,000	12½%	30	1	$576.51	$71,940.58
			2	619.75	73,588.44
			3	666.23	74,863.65
			4	716.20	75,672.50
			5	769.92	75,905.58
			6–30	827.66	0.00

Growing Equity Mortgage (GEM)

This mortgage has a twist that allows your equity in the house to increase faster. You pay a bit more each year and that extra amount is applied directly to repayment of the debt principal. The increase in your payments is a predetermined percentage that is typically 7½% each year. Of course, with this type of increase, your debt will be paid off in considerably less than the originally scheduled 30 years, usually in 15 to 17 years.

One disadvantage of the GEM is that you lose your interest payment tax deduction faster than if you had paid off the debt more slowly. The advantages and disadvantages of early payoffs will be discussed in Chapter 18.

Price Level Adjustable Mortgage

A price level adjustable mortgage is a type of ARM in which your interest payments theoretically remain constant in terms of real buying power. Monthly payments are adjusted according to an inflation index such as the Consumer Price Index, with the added cost of inflation tacked on to the principal of the loan. So interest rates aren't changed at all, but your principal changes.

The problem with this type of mortgage is that if inflation soars, your monthly payments could reach beyond your means, unless the deal includes a payment cap. Once again, the problem of negative amortization makes this mortgage a less attractive choice.

Refinancing Blend

You may be lucky enough to come across a lender who, while not letting you assume the existing mortgage on a house, will work out a blended rate for you. Unlike the blended mortgages we spoke harshly of earlier, the refinancing blend is an excellent opportunity, if you can find it.

What the lender will do is combine the interest

rate on the existing mortgage with the current rate, to come up with a compromise rate that is less than the current one, but greater than the old. For example, if the old rate is 6%, and the current rate is 11%, the lender might blend the two of them together and offer you a rate of, say, 9%. Definitely better than paying 11%.

Blending gives the lender an advantage because it gets the older-rate mortgage off its books.

Rollover Mortgage

Also known as a renegotiable rate mortgage, this is really a long-term loan that is renegotiated in full at prearranged intervals of usually 3 or 5 years. It works similarly to an ARM in that the maximum that the interest rate can be raised is predetermined. Be sure to understand how fees or points for the new loan will be calculated.

Shared Appreciation Mortgage

In this type of mortgage, the lender will offer you a lower initial rate of interest in exchange for a share in the appreciation (increase) in value of the house over a certain number of years.

Most lenders are reluctant to enter into this type of deal, because it offers them a negative cash flow and because they do not have a guarantee that the property will, in fact, appreciate in value. It's also a highly uncertain arrangement for the buyer, since at a certain point in the future you may owe a large lump sum to the lender which would probably require refinancing your mortgage. We would avoid this approach unless you desperately need the lower initial interest rate.

Shared Equity Mortgage

In a shared equity situation, two or more people, relatives, friends or even strangers, share in the ownership of a property. One or more of them is given the right to live in the house, and all share in the payments and are able to take their pro rata portion of the tax advantages. When the house is sold, each party receives his or her proportionate share of the proceeds.

The most common shared equity situation occurs when parents help their children by giving them the money needed for a down payment, in exchange for a share in the ownership of the property. However, more and more people are entering into shared equity arrangements with strangers.

Wraparound Mortgage

The wraparound is often used by lenders when old loans are assumable. In a wraparound, the buyer assumes the old mortgage loan, and the new money that the buyer needs to pay off the seller is added to the old loan, but at current rates. So, it is said that the new loan "wraps around" the old one. These loans are almost always with one bank. Ask the seller who their mortgage is with and if it's a bank you are considering, ask the banker about it.

11

APPLYING FOR A MORTGAGE

Once you have decided which type of mortgage you want and which lender will give it to you, it is time to apply for the loan. This need not be a great trauma, if you know what to expect.

The mortgage lender will ask a number of questions and will require a copy of your agreement of sale. You will have to pay for a credit check (usually $25 or $30). You will also have to pay for having the house appraised by the lender (usually $125 to $200).

Credit Check

It's a good idea to go to a local credit bureau prior to applying for the mortgage and pay for a credit check on yourself. This will give you the opportunity to correct any errors that appear on the report. It will also alert you to any potential problems in your credit history that have to be explained to the mortgage lender. See the No Nonsense Financial Guide, *How to Use Credit and Credit Cards*.

Be Frank

It is always best to bring up these potential problems yourself and to explain them prior to the issue of a credit report. By being forthright with the lender, you establish a good climate and you take the edge off potentially damaging information.

You will also have to fill out a form providing complete information regarding your earning ability and potential, and that of your spouse or other wage earner who will occupy the dwelling.

A sample mortgage application form is included in Appendix A. Also included are samples of forms used to apply for VA and FHA mortgages.

Remember that lenders cannot discriminate against you because of race, religion, color, national origin, or, in states that have an Equal Rights Amendment, sex.

28%/36%

The lender will do a computation of your net worth, earning potential and the amount they feel you can carry in monthly mortgage payments. Most lenders follow the 28/36 rule.

The 28% portion of the formula means that your maximum monthly payment for housing cannot be more than 28% of the gross monthly income of all the wage earners in the house. The 36% portion means that the total of *all* monthly debt payments, including the mortgage, cannot be greater than 36% of the gross monthly income of all the wage earners.

What to Do If You Are Turned Down

If you don't get the mortgage—don't despair. You can always try another lender, or increase your down payment. Perhaps a relative will lend you some money for a down payment, or you can try shared equity.

One other suggestion might not be easy, but it is worth mentioning. You could try to reduce your other indebtedness in order to improve your 28/36 ratio. Finally, you should consider the other types of mortgage loans that might be easier for you to get—for example, the graduated payment mortgage where the initial payments are lower, so that you can qualify with a lower income.

12

DOWN PAYMENTS—SMALL OR LARGE?

The question of the size of the down payment is a tricky one, depending on many factors.

Advantages of a Small Down Payment

When you buy a house with a small down payment, you are taking advantage of a financial trick called *leveraging*. This means that by using a small amount of your own money you are able to make a large purchase, in this case a house.

Leveraging works for you because it propels your small investment into the potential for greatness, that is ultimate home ownership. If you have little cash available, leveraging is essential. If you have more cash, leveraging prevents you from having to tie it all up in a nonliquid investment—that is, one that you cannot easily convert into cash on short notice.

Because you have not invested all your money in the house, you still have the money to invest in other investments such as stocks, mutual funds, etc. Or you can keep your money in a bank or money market fund for use the minute you need it.

Advantages of a Large Down Payment

On the other hand, you are in a better bargaining position to get a good deal on a mortgage if your down payment is substantial. You will probably have less trouble obtaining the mortgage of your choice, and the amount of your mortgage loan will be smaller.

Your equity in the house will be immediately greater with a large down payment, and, if your down payment is 20% or so, you will not have to spend extra money to purchase mortgage insurance. (See Chapter 13.)

Which to Choose

Assuming that all other factors are equal, and that you will be able to get financing with either a small or a large down payment, which one should you choose? That depends entirely on your economic situation. Think of other ways you might want or need to spend the money. Are any big expenses coming up in the near future? College costs or vacations, for example?

You should also consider how much money your extra dollars might earn in other investments, compared with locking them up in your house. Estimate what the investments might earn per year. Then figure out what the difference would be in your annual mortgage payments, between a large and a small down payment. This should help to clarify the issue.

13

MORTGAGE INSURANCE

Many lenders of non-government backed loans require the buyer to purchase private mortgage insurance (PMI). Private mortgage insurance should not be confused with mortgage *life* insurance, discussed later in this chapter. The purpose of PMI is to guarantee that if you default on the mortgage payments, the lender will get back the full balance of the loan.

If your down payment is less than 10% of the cost of the house, your lender will almost certainly require you to get mortgage insurance. Insurance will also probably be required if your down payment is between 10% and 20% and your mortgage note is being resold to one of the secondary mortgage markets we spoke of in Chapter 4.

The largest writer of mortgage insurance is the Mortgage Guarantee Insurance Company, known as MGIC (pronounced "magic"). This Milwaukee company was founded in 1957, and has, for most of the time since then, dominated the business. But mortgage insurance is also written by many other companies and is sometimes provided by the lender itself.

Mortgage insurance costs have remained rather steady over time, averaging about $5 for every $1,000 of first year coverage.

How PMI Payments Are Made

There are two common ways to pay for PMI. The choice is up to the buyer of the property. The first is to pay one lump sum at settlement. The amount charged for a lump sum payoff is regulated by each state and depends on the type of mortgage loan you have obtained. It generally is quite high, often 3½% of the borrowed amount. But a lump sum payoff has the advantage of avoiding all future PMI payments.

The second way is to pay for PMI monthly. This usually means that you will have to pay a flat fee for the first year PMI at settlement and monthly fees thereafter. The flat fee usually amounts to approximately 1% of the mortgage loan. How the remaining PMI payments are pro-rated depends on state regulation. In some states, PMI is only paid on the unpaid mortgage principal balance, a figure which continually declines. In other states, a level payment is made for the first 3, 5, or 10 years and then a lower payment is assessed for the remainder of the loan.

For example, with a 5% down payment and a fixed-rate mortgage loan for 95% of the sale price, you would need PMI. Let's assume a PMI rate of ¼ of 1% of the borrowed amount each year. In most states, you would have to pay a first year fee of 1% of the borrowed amount at settlement. Your yearly PMI payments would then be pro-rated, so that you paid ¹⁄₁₂ of the yearly sum each month as part of your regular mortgage payments.

You may be told that if you pay your PMI up front, you will be able to deduct it from your taxes because your lender will add it to the loan origination fee (see Chapter 14). This may be true and it may not be, depending on the state. Before you decide to prepay because of a potential tax break, we suggest that you consult your accountant or attorney.

Cancelling Mortgage Insurance

You really do not need mortgage insurance for the full life of your loan. It is quite understandable for a lender to want insurance when your equity in the property is small or nonexistent and the size of the loan is large relative to the value of the house. But as your equity increases and the loan is reduced, the lender is then fully protected by the value of the house, and you should not have to continue to pay for insurance. Accordingly, many of the private policies run for 5, 7, or 10 years—on the theory that that should be long enough.

Fannie Mae and Freddie Mac (see Chapter 4) have promulgated guidelines on cancelling mortgage insurance. However, not all lenders subscribe to the guidelines, and each lender sets its own rules. Under the Fannie/Freddie guidelines, insurance may be cancelled when the outstanding balance on the mortgage is less than 80% of the purchase price, or if the balance is less than 80% of a current acceptable appraised value.

How much will you save by cancelling insurance? It could be as much as $125 to $175 per year. So check the mortgage contract with your lender before signing and try to see that the insurance is required only for a limited period.

It is, of course, harder to cancel mortgage insurance when the lender is also the insurer. Many lenders are self-insurers and are reluctant to cancel policies that are bringing them money. But when your unpaid loan balance falls below 80% of the value of the property, try to cancel in any event.

Mortgage Life Insurance

Mortgage *life* insurance should not be confused with the private mortgage insurance discussed above. The purpose of mortgage life insurance, very simply, is to guarantee that the mortgage can be paid off if you die. You may be required to take out such insurance as part of the financing deal.

Mortgage life insurance is usually a form of *decreasing term* life insurance—the simplest and cheapest life insurance, with no savings element or cash value, and with the coverage decreasing each year to match the remaining principal amount of your mortgage. Again, you may be required to carry this insurance for the life of the mortgage, and again, the lender doesn't really need this protection after the first few years.

From the standpoint of your family, this coverage may not be at all a bad idea. The drawbacks are, first, that you very likely could have purchased the same term insurance more cheaply elsewhere. Second, this insurance will probably be made payable to the lender, who will use it automatically to pay off the mortgage if you die; if it were payable to your family, they might perhaps find it better to keep the mortgage alive and to use the insurance money in other ways. If you do have to take (or decide to take) mortgage life insurance, try to work out arrangements that will be best for you and your family.

14

ESCROW, POINTS AND OTHER CHARGES

This chapter is about a few important items for you to remember.

Escrow

Escrow is the holding by an impartial party of money deposited until certain conditions are met. In the case of the sale of a house, the escrow consists of the good faith deposit (also called the "earnest money") that the buyer makes to seal the deal. Until closing, the money is held *in escrow*—that is, on deposit—by an escrow agent agreed upon by the buyer and seller.

Make sure someone you trust, or an agreeable independent party, holds your escrow money. Your attorney or a nonbiased third party is a good choice. With new construction, the builder's lender is fine. You don't want your money held by the builder and commingled with that of other buyers. If your money is commingled and the builder goes bankrupt, you may never get your money back because it will be locked in as part of the bankruptcy.

Points

There are a number of charges that the mortgage lender may require you or the seller to pay at settlement (closing). These include *points*. Each point represents a one-time charge of 1% of the total amount of the mortgage loan. Points can cover specific cost items of the lender, or they can simply be a way for the lender to get more money from you without raising the stated interest rate.

One point is frequently charged for the title search and for insurance against nonpayment of taxes. Points can also be charged and called various things such as origination fees, placement fees, participation or commitment fees. These are all additional charges by the lender. Very frequently, one additional point is charged if your down payment is less than 20%.

Deductibility of Points

The deductibility of points on your income tax return is a tricky question. When you buy a new home, you can usually take an immediate tax deduction for points paid on your mortgage, as if the points represented an immediate payment of interest. The rule states that an immediate deduction is permitted if the points are paid in connection with the *purchase* of your *principal residence*. In refinancing, however, where you already own the property, the IRS tells you to spread the deduction for points over the life of the mortgage loan— obviously a less favorable arrangement.

An immediate deduction also is permitted if points are paid on a loan to be used for *improvement* of your principal residence. In this case, payment of points must be standard practice in your area and the number of points you pay must not be excessive, in order for you to qualify for an immediate deduction. As these rules are complicated, we suggest that you consult your tax attorney or accountant. There has been some talk in Congress of making *all* points immediately deductible, and a change in the law is a possibility.

Buy-Down

The builder of a new house (or sometimes the seller of an older one, or the buyer himself or herself) may buy-down the mortgage for the buyer. This means that the builder will pay the lender the cash equivalent of one or

51

several points of interest so that the buyer has a lower interest rate to pay on the mortgage loan. Buy-downs are excellent deals for buyers, who benefit directly from the reduction in mortgage payments which, in effect, becomes a discount on the sale price.

A buy-down can be either permanent or temporary. In a permanent buy-down, the seller pays the cash equivalent of interest points for the life of the loan. The following table shows the cost of permanent buy-downs on a 30-year mortgage:

| | Amount of Mortgage | | |
	$40,000	$70,000	$100,000
Buy-down of ½% (from 10% to 9½%)	1,673	2,930	4,184
Buy-down of 1% (from 10% to 9%)	3,325	5,819	8,313
Buy-down of 1½% (from 10% to 8½%)	4,952	8,668	12,382

More prevalent is the temporary buy-down where the interest is reduced for a specified number of years. A common arrangement is to buy-down 3% in the first year of the mortgage, 2% in the second, and 1% in the third.

Settlement or Closing

Settlement (also called closing) can be a trauma, but it need not be, if you're prepared and do your homework.

What is Settlement

Settlement is the time when the buyer becomes the actual owner of the property. Many documents are signed and much money changes hands.

Be Prepared

Bring extra checks with you, several pens, and a calculator to check the numbers. Bring all your documents with you and check the final papers against your preliminary drafts for any discrepancies. It is a good idea to take your attorney with you so that any problems that arise can be settled on the spot.

Good Faith Estimate

Within three days of applying for a mortgage loan, the lender must supply the borrower with a good faith estimate of settlement charges. This is according to the federal Real Estate Settlement Procedures Act (RESPA). A copy of the standard RESPA form is reproduced in Appendix B.

The Settlement Sheet

The *settlement sheet* is a document prepared at the settlement of a real estate purchase that details all the various charges paid to and by each party to the transaction. A sample of the HUD settlement sheet is reproduced in Appendix C.

Remember that there are different rules and customs relating to which party pays what settlement costs and the amount of the costs. You should check with your lender, attorney, and real estate agent to avoid any surprises. A general guideline is that settlement will probably cost the buyer about 5% of the sale price of the house.

There are often extra costs that might not show up on the good faith estimate, such as advance payment of taxes and utility bills. Some locales require the buyer to prepay one year of taxes at settlement in addition to the transfer taxes assessed by state and local governments. The buyer will also have to pay for mortgage insurance (see Chapter 13), title search and insurance, homeowner's insurance, survey and often attorney's fees, and adjustments.

As previously explained, many of these charges are expressed in terms of points, each point representing 1% of the face value of the mortgage. So, if the mortgage loan were for $50,000, one point would represent $500.

There will also probably be a mortgage loan origination fee. The lender is likely to charge between 1 and
4 points, or 1% to 4% of the borrowed amount. One
percent is most common. The origination fee is usually
paid by the buyer, but custom or agreement of the
parties could allow the seller to pay it, or for each of
the parties to pay one-half.

15

SPECIAL SITUATIONS—
FINANCING CONDOMINIUMS
AND CO-OPS

Many people today are buying into shared living situations, such as condominiums and cooperatives, because of the easy, maintenance-free lifestyle, the amenities, and the locations they offer. For more information on this subject, read the No Nonsense Real Estate Guide, *Understanding Condominiums and Co-ops.*

Condominiums

A condominium is a type of shared living where each person owns his or her unit in fee simple—that is, with the same type of complete and total ownership one gets in a house. In addition to owning the individual unit, the buyer also has an ownership share in all the common areas (known as *common elements*), such as lobby, elevators, parking, recreational facilities, etc. The amount of this share is usually determined according to the ratio of the size of the owner's individual unit compared with the total area of all the units in the development.

Because you actually own your condo unit, you can get a mortgage loan to finance its purchase. HUD loans are available for qualifying units. The amount of the mortgage loan you can get depends on the amount that you can afford (see Chapter 11 for the 28/36 rule), taking into account the fact that you will have to pay not only your monthly mortgage payment, but also a monthly assessment for maintenance of the common areas.

Since you actually have title to your unit, in fee simple, you can pledge your title to the lender. If you default, the lender can exercise his or her lien and foreclose.

Cooperatives

A cooperative is also a shared-space, joint living situation, but it differs from a condominium in several ways. In a co-op, you don't actually own the unit you live in. What you own is a number of shares in the coop corporation, a certain number of shares being allocated to each unit. The corporation owns the entire development—apartments, recreational facilities, elevators, etc.—and shareholders occupy individual units under a proprietary lease.

(Because a cooperative owner does not actually own his or her unit, the cooperative board has more power to interfere in your life, promulgating rules regarding such things as the manner in which you use your unit, to whom you can sell and if you can rent, have children, pets, etc.)

The cooperative corporation usually has taken out a mortgage loan on the entire development. You, as a shareholder, pay a pro rata portion of the mortgage loan each month as part of a monthly fee. This fee includes maintenance and upkeep as well as your share of the mortgage loan payments.

But because you don't actually own your co-op unit, you can't get a mortgage loan to cover your cost of purchase. So how do you finance a co-op? You get a personal loan, which in this case works similarly to a mortgage. It is usual for the rates on a co-op loan to be one or several points higher than the going rate on mortgage loans. This is because there is more uncertainty for the co-op lender, who holds your co-op shares as security, rather than an actual property such as a house or condo unit.

16

WHAT IF YOU CAN'T PAY THIS MONTH?

Hardly anything in life is more depressing than being unable to meet a regular mortgage payment. Yet the problem may be beyond your control—temporary unemployment, or emergency medical bills. In any case, don't panic. There are things you can do.

The first rule to follow is be up-front. Don't try to hide from the lender—remember that your lender knows you haven't paid, just as well as you know it.

Go immediately to the lender and explain the situation. Discuss the problem, and you will almost certainly be able to work out a repayment schedule together.

If your mortgage is FHA-insured or VA-guaranteed, call the agency immediately. They may be able to help. The Department of Housing and Urban Development (HUD) has a list of approved housing counseling agencies to contact. These counselors are experienced professionals who have helped many people avoid foreclosure.

Remember that foreclosure is a costly affair which most lenders regard as a last resort. Your lender would much rather work with you, if possible, than be forced to treat you as an adversary. If you have any reasonable prospect of getting back on a regular payment schedule, there's every likelihood that your lender will cooperate.

17

YOUR MORTGAGE AND THE TAX REFORM ACT OF 1986

One of the major changes made by the Tax Reform Act of 1986 is the treatment of deductions for interest payments. While the deduction for many types of interest payments is being phased out, interest on a home mortgage is still generally deductible. But there are limits.

First, the deduction for "qualified housing interest" under the 1986 law *is limited to interest on debt taken against a taxpayer's principal residence or second residence only.* If you are fortunate enough to have more than two residences—note this limitation.

Second, with the exceptions noted below, *the debt on which interest is deductible may not exceed the cost basis of the property*—the original purchase price plus the cost of any improvements.

When you take out a mortgage on a new home, the mortgage will ordinarily be for less than the cost of the property, and the cost basis limitation will not be a problem. However, when you are refinancing a mortgage, or taking out a second mortgage or a home equity loan on a residence that has risen in value, this limitation becomes significant.

The Importance of Cost Basis

Because of the cost basis limitation, you must keep careful track of the amount spent on improvements. If you bought your home for $80,000 and have since spent $4,000 for a finished basement and $8,000 for a new kitchen, your new cost basis will be $92,000, and you can deduct interest paid on a mortgage loan of up to $92,000.

In addition, if you paid any state or local tax on the purchase of your home, that tax can be included as part of your cost basis under the new law.

(**Note:** *if you refinanced your mortgage or took out a new mortgage before August 17, 1986,* the amount of the mortgage can be up to the *fair market value* of the property, and the interest will still be fully deductible, even if the fair market value exceeds the cost basis.)

The Educational-Medical Exception

There is another intriguing exception to the cost basis rule: The debt can exceed your cost basis to the extent it is incurred for educational or medical expenses, and the interest will still be deductible. (The educational expenses may include reasonable living expenses away from home for students from primary through graduate school.)

What is a Residence?

Note that the tax law specifically defines "residence" for the purpose of the mortgage deduction. Specifically, if one of your homes, such as a vacation home, is rented out part of the time, mortgage interest will be fully deductible as "qualified residence interest" only if you use the home personally for the *greater* of (a) 14 days or (b) 10% of the number of days for which the home is rented out. Otherwise, the mortgage interest will be considered as an expense of the rental activity, and it will be deductible only against other rental or similar income.

And the debt must be on a *residence*. This means that if you own land on which you hope someday to build a vacation home, any interest you pay on a loan against that land will not be deductible as long as no residence has yet been built on the land.

Cooperatives

Loans on cooperatives qualify for the interest deduction, even though they are not, technically speaking, mortgages on real estate.

Borrowing For More Than Your Cost Basis

Should you ever borrow for more than your tax basis, so that part of the mortgage interest you pay will not be tax deductible? Yes—if you need to borrow a substantial amount, borrowing on your home may be the only practical way to do it. And whatever the size of the borrowing, interest rates on loans secured by your home are generally considerably lower than other consumer interest rates. Moreover, the tax deduction on other forms of consumer interest is being phased out under the 1986 law, so that the alternatives to mortgage borrowing may not be very attractive. (For more information on the Tax Reform Act of 1986, see the No Nonsense Financial Guide, *The New Tax Law and What It Means To You.*)

But Beware of Borrowing Unwisely

The real danger we see in the new tax law is that borrowing against your home may have become *too* attractive. Considering the tax advantage, the lower interest rates on home borrowings compared with other types of loans, and the easy availability of second mortgages and home equity credit lines, it's almost a certainty that many people will borrow excessively against their homes without considering the dangers. If you are tempted to refinance or obtain a home equity loan for more than you really need, think not twice but three times. Remember that extra debt should not be entered into casually. You will have to repay the money you borrow, with interest. *And your home is pledged as security for the loan.* Don't take this extra risk without good reason.

18

MANAGING YOUR MORTGAGE— PREPAYMENT

If you are an average American, buying a house may be the biggest single investment you will ever make, and taking out a mortgage may be the biggest single borrowing you will ever do.

If your income is limited, it may be all you can do to meet the mortgage payments, and at first the mortgage may feel like a financial burden. But with time, or with added income, the situation may change—all the more so if the house has appreciated in value.

Look at your situation in a new way. You are the owner of a valuable asset—your house. This asset has given you substantial borrowing power which you would not have had otherwise. You can *manage* this borrowing in ways that will do you the most good. If the interest rate is too high, you can try to reduce it. If you are uncomfortable with the size of the debt, you can consider paying off part or even all of it. If the value of your house is well above the balance of your loan—either because your house has risen in value, or because you have paid down the loan—you can change your borrowing arrangements in one of several ways to borrow *more*, making your asset work for you.

Many people believe that debt is bad, and feel uncomfortable with it. There's no reason to think that way if the borrowing is for a legitimate purpose, and certainly home ownership is an excellent one. Some features of the economic system make debt an advantage. With debt, you can own an asset (such as a house) that will rise in value with inflation, while the amount of the debt is fixed and doesn't rise. The interest payments you make on your mortgage, as we have seen, are still generally tax deductible.

However, a mortgage does give a lender a claim against your house, and you may feel happier if you pay off the mortgage faster. If the mortgage carries a high interest rate, there's every reason to try to pay it off earlier or to refinance (see Chapter 19).

Do the Mathematics

Your feelings may be as important as the mathematics, but you should do the mathematics first to know where you stand.

Let's say you have accumulated enough savings to pay down your mortgage balance by a certain amount, or that your income has risen so that you could afford to make higher monthly payments. Consider your mortgage interest rate. What rate do you think you could earn on the money if you invested it elsewhere? If you are paying off an old 8% mortgage, and you are currently earning 9% on the money in a money market fund, using the savings to reduce the debt would actually reduce your income. But if the numbers are reversed—let's say you have a 14% mortgage—then paying down the debt would improve your monthly cash position.

Consider the Future

Of course, you have to consider what your savings might earn in the future as well as the present. And if you have an ARM, you also have to consider how your mortgage interest rate might change in the future. You may not be able to make a precise calculation, but at least you will know roughly whether prepaying part of the debt will save you current dollars or not.

Prepayment Penalty

Then you have to consider other factors. Almost all mortgage contracts permit prepayment of part or all of the outstanding balance, but there may be a penalty.

In some cases, the penalty for prepayment of the whole balance might be as much as six months' interest—a big bite. Obviously, you are better off if you can originally obtain a mortgage loan that doesn't carry prepayment penalties.

Flexibility

Remember that even if there's no penalty, you retain more flexibility by *not* prepaying your loan. Prepayment is a one-way street. As long as you hold your cash, invest it elsewhere, and don't prepay, you still have open the choice of prepaying whenever you wish. But once you have used cash to pay down the loan balance, you can't reverse the process and get the cash back without going through the costly process of renegotiating your mortgage. So don't think twice, think three times before deciding on prepayment. A mortgage loan is a valuable financial tool which you went through much trouble to get. If the mortgage carries good terms, don't give any part of it away quickly.

Conclusion

Still, you may have completely legitimate reasons for prepaying part or all of your debt. The flexibility factor may not be that important to you. You may have made a hard dollar calculation and decided that paying off the mortgage is the best investment you could make with your cash, and that you could not do better by investing it elsewhere. You may not trust yourself as a financial manager, and you may be much happier paying off the mortgage and owning the house free and clear. If you are close to retirement, you may feel more secure knowing that the mortgage payments are behind you, and that if you run into financial difficulties your house will not be at risk. If you are involved in planning your estate, you may want to know that your spouse or children can inherit the house free and clear.

So do the math first, but remember that the right decision is the one that will make you happiest over the long run.

19

MANAGING YOUR MORTGAGE—
REFINANCING

There are many reasons why you might want to refinance your mortgage—which means, in effect, replacing it with a different mortgage. You may feel that you can save money by getting a new mortgage at a lower interest rate. Or you may want to stretch out the payment schedule. Or you may have built up your equity in the house—either because the house has risen in value, or because you have paid down the mortgage substantially—and now you wish to borrow more so that you can use the additional cash for other purposes.

Reducing Interest

One of the most common motives for refinancing is to take advantage of lower interest rates. Let's say that you took out a 14% mortgage in 1980, when interest rates were dancing in the stratosphere. Now you can get a similar mortgage at 10%. What should you do?

Before you even talk to your mortgage lender, you must do a careful calculation of the saving on monthly interest costs. Take into account the tax deduction that you get on interest payments; and remember that if you intend to refinance for a larger amount, your interest payments might not be fully deductible (see Chapter 17). Below is a table showing the savings you will achieve (disregarding the tax factor) by refinancing your 30-year, 14% mortgage at various interest rates:

Amount of Mortgage		Interest Rate on New Mortgage					
	14%	12%	11%	10%	9%	8%
$ 40,000						
monthly payment	$ 473.95	$ 441.45	$ 380.93	$ 351.03	$ 321.85	$ 293.51
monthly savings	—	62.50	93.02	122.92	152.10	180.44
70,000						
monthly payment	829.41	720.03	666.63	614.30	563.24	513.64
monthly savings	—	109.38	162.78	215.11	266.17	315.77
100,000						
monthly payment	1184.87	1028.61	952.32	877.57	804.62	733.77
monthly savings	—	156.26	232.55	307.30	380.25	451.10

You must balance these savings against the costs of refinancing to see how many months it will take for your monthly net interest savings to make up for the immediate cash loss.

How Much Does Refinancing Cost?

It's difficult to say precisely how much refinancing will cost, because the charges vary from state to state and according to your individual situation. But it could cost plenty, and that's why refinancing should not be undertaken lightly. You will have another closing to attend and, at worst, may have to go through all the same procedures and costs you originally incurred in getting a mortgage loan—credit check, appraisal, title search, origination fees, filing fees, attorney's costs, etc. And, if your old mortgage carries a prepayment penalty (see Chapter 18), you will have to pay it in addition to the other costs. So, refinancing can be expensive, and you must find out precisely what will be involved before you make a final decision.

Negotiate

Some costs can be eliminated or reduced if you present your refinancing case properly. Remember that you now are in a position to negotiate because you have equity in your house. And, if the new mortgage is to be with the same lender, and if the change is one the lender wants—for example, if you want to increase the amount of your mortgage, and if your credit and record at the bank are good—then the lender may let you short-cut some of the costs.

If you plan to stay with your old lender, but the change is one that benefits you and not the lender, you can expect to be hit with whatever charges the lender is permitted to impose, unless you can convince him or her that the change is not as bad as it seems. But if your old lender won't give you the deal you want, and if you intend to take out a new mortgage loan with a new lender, then most of the costs may be hard to avoid.

Negotiating Tools

Let's say that you do your business banking at the Bigelow Bank but you have your home mortgage with the Rainbow Valley Bank and you are thinking of refinancing. Bigelow Bank may want to consolidate your account and may offer you a better deal on refinancing than Rainbow Valley. But what about Rainbow Valley? What if you move your personal and business banking to them, in exchange for a refinancing break? We're not saying that this is a sure way to reduce charges, but it often works, so you should have your negotiating battle plan figured out before you approach any lenders.

A General Rule To Follow

Every case works out differently, but a rule of thumb is that the refinancing will only be worthwhile if the difference in interest rates is at least 3%, and if you will be living in the house and paying off the new mortgage for at least two years. But try to do the math, and see how the rule works out in your own case. For more details about refinancing, see the No Nonsense Real Estate Guide, *Refinancing Your Mortgage*.

20

MANAGING YOUR MORTGAGE— SECOND MORTGAGES AND HOME EQUITY LOANS

We have seen that one possible reason for refinancing is to boost the size of your mortgage and take out extra cash. But what if you want to generate extra cash without refinancing?

Refinancing may be pointless if you are still carrying a substantial balance on a pre-1979 mortgage, at an interest rate lower than you could obtain today. Or, if you are not worried about interest rates rising in the future, you may have an ARM that you consider attractive and that you are content to keep.

If your mortgage was for a low percentage of cost in the first place, or if it has been paid down to an amount well below your cost basis, you can borrow an additional amount up to the cost basis and still deduct the interest for tax purposes. (See Chapter 17.)

In many cases, the fair market value of your home has appreciated to far more than the original cost. You may be able to borrow up to about 80% of this fair market value. In this situation, the interest on the amount borrowed *above the cost basis* will not be tax deductible. However, you will generally be borrowing at interest rates considerably lower than other consumer interest rates. (And note the educational-medical exception. See Chapter 17.)

There are two common ways of borrowing additional amounts on your home—a second mortgage or a home equity credit line.

More information about second mortgages and

home equity loans can be found in the No Nonsense Real Estate Guide, *Refinancing Your Mortgage.*

Second Mortgages

A second mortgage is an additional mortgage loan that you take out based on the equity you own in your home. Rather than refinancing, you keep the first mortgage and add another mortgage to it. The second mortgage lender has a lien on your home, just as the first mortgage lender, but the second is junior to the first; in case of foreclosure, the second mortgage lender must wait until the primary lender is paid off in full before he or she can collect.

A disadvantage of second mortgages is that interest rates generally are higher than on first mortgages, because of the junior position the second lender must assume. And initial costs are usually the same as for any refinancing. But second mortgages can be a viable method of obtaining needed cash in some circumstances. Most second mortgages are fixed-rate loans, but some lenders also offer variable-rate arrangements. (Remember that in a variable-rate arrangement, you, the borrower, bear much of the interest rate risk, which may be substantial.)

Home Equity Loans

Another way of borrowing on your equity without refinancing is the home equity loan, which is really a newer and more flexible form of second mortgage.

Home equity loans are the latest and "hottest" way of unlocking the extra credit power in your house. Banks, savings and loans, brokerage firms, mortgage bankers, and finance companies have all jumped on this new bandwagon.

The Cost

Though the advertisements don't stress the fact, setting up this sort of credit arrangement may cost money. In most cases, the lender puts you through a full mortgage check (appraisal, credit check, etc.) and recording, title insurance, points, and other fees may have to be paid, just as on a regular mortgage. However, when the competition for home equity loans is keen, lenders may waive all or some of these charges; so it pays to compare several loan sources.

Varieties of Home Equity Loans

Home equity loans come in three basic varieties. The first is similar to a second mortgage in that a lump sum is borrowed and paid back over a specified period of time with either a fixed or a floating interest rate. The fixed-rate repayment schedule is preferable if the interest rate is reasonable. The floating-rate arrangement is similar to an ARM (see Chapter 9), and carries similar risks if interest rates rise over the course of repayment.

The second type is a revolving charge, usually called a home equity line of credit. The line is set up with a certain maximum amount of money available. You can tap into the line whenever you wish, either all at once, or in smaller doses. You pay interest only on the actual amount borrowed, but you pay the charges for setting up the line whether or not you use it. There may or may not be a fixed repayment schedule—some lenders permit you to keep a debt balance indefinitely as long as you maintain regular interest payments. More typical is a repayment schedule of 10 years (120 months). Interest rates can either be fixed or floating; again, we stress that a fixed rate is preferable, but the typical home equity credit line carries a floating rate.

A third type of home equity loan is used mainly by professionals who draw compensation from their firms only once or twice a year. This type of loan must be paid back completely by a certain date each year. The *annual clearance* feature of the loan makes it practical only for people with this type of special borrowing need.

How Much Can You Borrow?

The amount you can borrow under the above arrangements is best shown by an example. Let's say that your house is appraised at $120,000, and the lender's practice is to lend up to 80% of the appraised value. In your case that amounts to $96,000. But you still owe a balance of $60,000 on your mortgage. The lender subtracts $60,000 from $96,000 and arrives at $36,000, which is the net amount available for you to borrow. (Of course, if $96,000 is greater than your cost basis, not all the interest you pay will be tax deductible. (See Chapter 17.)

Some Pitfalls

Home equity loans can be useful. But there are a few important warnings. First, make sure you understand all the rules and costs. What will you be charged for the initial appraisal and the other costs of setting up the loan or credit line? Will you have to repeat the whole procedure at the end of 5 years, or whenever the initial period expires? How will the interest rate be figured? On what schedule will repayments be due?

Second, remember that if you have a floating interest rate—as is true with most equity lines of credit—the interest rate you pay will adjust periodically according to some index, such as the bank's prime loan rate. And ordinarily *there's no cap* on the interest rate you may have to pay. If interest rates generally rise, you may be stuck with higher interest rates whether you can afford them or not. And if you want to repay your loan early, be aware that some equity lines with a fixed repayment schedule carry a prepayment penalty.

Finally, don't enter into a home equity loan without remembering that *the lender has a lien on your house.* This isn't just a personal loan—it's the equivalent of a mortgage. So even if the interest rate will be lower than on a personal loan, *make sure that you can repay what you borrow before you put your house at risk.*

GLOSSARY

Abstract of Title A record of the title, or history of ownership, of a property.

Adjustable Mortgage Loan (AML) Similar to an ARM, and offered by savings and loan associations. See Adjustable Rate Mortgage.

Adjustable Rate Mortgage (ARM) A mortgage whose interest rate is periodically adjusted according to an agreed-upon index.

Agreement of Sale The legal contract between the buyer and the seller of a property including the sale price, settlement date, and all conditions and terms of the sale.

Amortization The process by which the principal amount of a loan is reduced through periodic repayments.

Appraisal An expert evaluation of the fair market value of a property.

Appreciation An increase in value of a property.

Assumable Mortgage A mortgage that can be taken over on its original terms by a subsequent buyer of the house. All FHA and VA mortgages are assumable.

Attorney's Opinion of Title An Abstract of Title.

Attorney's Record Search and Opinion See Abstract of Title.

Balloon Mortgage A type of mortgage loan where monthly payments are made until a certain date when the remaining balance becomes payable in full.

Blended Mortgage An ill-advised scheme for fooling the mortgage lender in situations where the existing mortgage is not assumable.

Bridge Loan See Swing Loan.

Buy-down A procedure by which the seller or builder of a house permanently or temporarily reduces the amount of interest the buyer will have to pay by paying points to the mortgage lender at closing.

Buyer-Agent An agent hired and paid for by the buyer of a property to find the appropriate property and negotiate for its purchase.

Call Option The right of a mortgage lender to require that the entire sum due and owing be paid because of the occurrence of a specified event.

Cap A limit on how much the monthly payments or interest rate can vary in an Adjustable Rate Mortgage.

Closing The time when legal title to a property passes from the seller to the buyer. (Also termed Settlement.)

Cloud on a Title See Defect in Title.

Collateral The security for repayment of a loan. In a mortgage loan, the property is pledged (mortgaged) as security.

Computerized Mortgage Networks Organizations which originate mortgage loans through the use of computers.

Condominium (Condo) A form of joint property ownership. Title to a specific condo unit is held in fee simple, with common elements jointly owned by all condo owners together.

Contract Sale (Contract for Deed) A type of sale of property where the title to the property does not pass until the seller has paid all amounts due on the existing mortgage with money furnished by the buyer. This type of sale deprives the buyer of protection because title does not pass until the conclusion of the contract.

Conventional Mortgage Loan Any mortgage loan that does not have government backing.

Co-operative (Co-op) A form of joint property ownership where the entire development is owned by a co-operative corporation whose shareholders have the right to occupy individual units.

Deed The piece of paper filed according to law which evidences title (ownership) of a property.

Deed of Trust A loan instrument used in some states in lieu of a mortgage.

Defect in Title A problem with the title to a property which renders the title not marketable.

Down Payment Cash payable by the buyer of a property equal to the difference between the total sale price and the amount of the mortgage loan, usually between 5% and 20% of the sale price.

Due-On-Sale Clause A provision in a mortgage contract providing for the entire sum of money due and owing to be paid immediately, upon the occurrence of certain conditions.

Earnest Money The deposit given by the buyer to the seller to show serious intent to purchase.

Easement The right to enter or use a portion of the land of another for a specific purpose.

Elastic Mortgage A type of mortgage loan where the amount of each mortgage payment remains constant, but the number of payments required may vary.

Equitable Owner The person who has signed an agreement of sale for a property but who does not as yet hold legal title to it.

Equity or Owner's Equity The amount by which the present market value of a property exceeds the amount of the mortgage and all other debts, claims or liens against the property.

Escrow Money deposited and held by a neutral third party in contemplation of a purchase.

Farmers Home Administration (FmHA) A part of the U.S. Department of Agriculture offering mortgage loans to farmers and non-farmers in qualifying rural areas.

Federal Home Loan Mortgage Corporation (Freddie Mac) A quasi-governmental agency which purchases mortgages from the original mortgage lenders.

Federal Housing Authority (FHA) A part of the U.S. Department of Housing and Urban Development which offers mortgage loan insurance programs to buyers of qualifying properties.

Federal National Mortgage Association (Fannie Mae) A quasi-governmental agency, now publicly owned, which purchases mortgages from the original mortgage lenders.

Fee Simple Absolute (Fee) The best and most complete form of legal ownership, carrying the absolute right to use, sell, or bequeath property in any manner desired.

Foreclosure The legal remedy used by a mortgage lender to assume ownership of a property when required loan repayments are not made.

Good Faith Deposit See Earnest Money.

Government National Mortgage Association (Ginnie Mae) A government agency, carrying the full faith and credit of the United States government, which purchases mortgages from the original mortgage lender.

Graduated Payment Mortgage A type of mortgage loan where the repayments start small and gradually increase.

Growing Equity Mortgage A type of mortgage loan where, in addition to periodic payments of principal and interest, additional payments are made to reduce the principal more quickly and increase the borrower's equity in the property.

HUD The U.S. Department of Housing and Urban Development.

Joint Tenants A form of property ownership between two

or more persons with "right of survivorship," where all can use and enjoy the whole property, and on death the whole property is owned by the survivor(s).

Leverage Using a small amount of money (capital) to obtain ownership and/or control of a large property.

Lien A legal notice, filed according to law, of the right of a lien holder (such as a mortgage lender) to be paid from the proceeds of the sale of property on which the lien was recorded.

Liquid Investment An investment that can be turned into cash easily and quickly.

Margin In an ARM, the spread between the interest rate in the index and the rate actually charged to the borrower.

Mortgage The legal document representing a loan of money in return for the pledge of property as collateral for the repayment of the loan with interest.

Mortgage Commitment The written notice from a mortgage lender that your mortgage application has been approved and that for a specified time period the mortgage loan will be available for you to buy a specified property.

Mortgagee The person or company who receives the mortgage as a pledge for repayment of the loan. The mortgage lender.

Mortgagor The mortgage borrower who gives the mortgage as a pledge to repay.

Multiple Listing Service (MLS) A service where house listings of member real estate agents are made available for all agents to sell. Commissions from multiple listing sales are split between co-operating agents.

Negative Amortization The process of adding to the principal balance of a loan when current payments do not fully cover the required interest.

Origination Fee A fee, usually amounting to one to four points (1% to 4% of the amount of the mortgage loan), charged by a mortgage lender at the inception of the loan.

Points Charges levied by the mortgage lender and usually payable at closing. One point represents 1% of the face value of the mortgage loan.

Prepayment Penalty A charge imposed by a mortgage lender on a borrower who wants to pay off part or all of a mortgage loan in advance of schedule.

Price Level Adjustment Mortgage A type of mortgage loan where the principal and the payments are adjusted upward periodically for inflation.

Principal The face amount borrowed in a mortgage loan.

Punch List A list compiled by the buyer during the pre-settlement inspection, detailing all defects and problems found in the property. The list is signed by the buyer and co-signed by the builder or his or her representative.

Real Estate Agent An employee of a real estate broker who has passed an examination and is licensed by the state.

Real Estate Broker A person who has passed an advanced examination and is licensed by the state to show houses to potential buyers and to negotiate purchases and sales, and to receive fees for such services.

Realtor See Real Estate Broker.

Refinancing Blend A mortgage loan where the lender blends the interest rate on an existing mortgage with the current interest rate in order to arrive at a rate which is more favorable to the borrower.

Renegotiable Rate Mortgage See Rollover Mortage.

Rollover Mortgage A mortgage loan which is renegotiated at periodic intervals.

Settlement See Closing.

Shared Appreciation Mortgage A mortgage loan where the mortgage lender offers a lower interest rate in exchange for subsequently being paid a part of the market appreciation of the property.

Shared Equity Mortgage An arrangement where two or more people pay for and share the ownership and tax advantages of a property.

Survey A legally precise description of a property including the location and size of the land and all buildings thereon.

Swing Loan A temporary loan obtained when you are buying one property before you sell another.

Tenants by the Entireties The legal form of ownership of property jointly by husband and wife.

Tenants in Common A form of property ownership where two or more persons own a property and all can use or enjoy it and each tenant can will, sell or devise his or her piece as desired (no right of survivorship).

Title Legal evidence of ownership of a property.

Title Company A company which researches titles and usually also insures them against defects.

Title Insurance Insurance obtained by the buyer of a house to insure against any undiscovered problems regarding the title to the property.

Title Search An investigation into the history of ownership of a property to check for liens, unpaid claims, restrictions or problems, to prove that the seller can transfer free and clear ownership.

Variable Rate Mortgage See Adjustable Rate Mortage.

Veterans Administration (VA) A government agency guaranteeing mortgage loans with no down payment to qualified veterans.

Warranty A protection plan for the repair or replacement of defective merchandise or workmanship.

Wraparound Mortgage A situation where the existing mortgage loan is assumed and the rest of the money needed to consummate the purchase is obtained from the same lender in the form of an additional mortgage which is said to "wrap around" the first.

Appendix A—Part I
APPLICATION FOR ALL CONVENTIONAL MORTGAGES

Federal National Mortgage Association

TRANSMITTAL SUMMARY

IDENTIFICATION

1 LOAN TYPE	2 APPROVAL REQUESTED	3 SUBMISSION TYPE
1 ☐ Conventional - SFPM 3 ☐ VA 2 ☐ Conventional - RRM	1 ☐ Property Only 2 ☐ Property and Credit 3 ☐ Credit (Property Previously Approved)	1 ☐ Prior Approval 3 ☐ Delegated Underwriting 2 ☐ Approval and Purchase

4 SUBMISSION NUMBER	5 PROPERTY ADDRESS
	(Street Number) (Street Name) (Section) (Unit)

6 CITY	7 STATE	8 ZIP CODE	9 PROJECT TYPE	10 PROJECT NO.
			1 ☐ PUD 3 ☐ DeMinimis PUD 2 ☐ Condo 4 ☐ Subdivision	

11 BORROWER	12 CO-BORROWER
(Last Name) (Initials)	(Last Name) (Initials)

PROPOSED FINANCING

13 MORTGAGE TYPE	14 MORTGAGE AMOUNT	15 GUARANTY AMOUNT (VA Only)	16 UNGUARANTEED PORTION (VA Only)	17 LOAN/VALUE RATIO	18 INTEREST RATE	19 ORIGINAL TERM
1 ☐ First Mortgage 2 ☐	$	$	% of Value			(Mos)

PROPERTY

20 NUMBER OF UNITS	21 SALE PRICE	22 APPRAISED VALUE	23 REASONABLE VALUE (VA Only)	24 VALUE
	$	$	$	$

STABLE MONTHLY INCOME / PROPOSED MONTHLY PAYMENTS

	BORROWER	CO-BORROWER	TOTAL			
25 BASE INCOME	$ _____	$ _____	$ _____	39	FIRST MORTGAGE P&I	$ _____
26 (OTHER)	_____	_____	_____	40	OTHER FINANCING	_____
27 (OTHER)	_____	_____	_____	41	HAZARD INSURANCE	_____
28 TOTAL INCOME	$ _____	$ _____	$ _____	42	TAXES	_____
				43	MORTGAGE INSURANCE	_____

INCOME RATIOS - SINGLE FAMILY

29 PAYMENT/INCOME RATIO	_____ %	44 HOME OWNER ASSN. FEES	_____
30 OBLIGATIONS/INCOME RATIO	_____ %	45 OTHER	_____

INCOME RATIOS - 2-4 FAMILY

31 EFFECTIVE GROSS INCOME	$ _____	46 TOTAL PAYMENT	$ _____
32 TOTAL OPERATING EXPENSES	(_____)	47 ALL OTHER MONTHLY PAYMENTS BEYOND 10 MONTHS (Including Applicable Alimony/Child Support)	
33 OPERATING INCOME Subject Property (Line 31 Less Line 32)	$ _____		
34 25% OF LINE 28	$ _____	48 TOTAL ALL MONTHLY PAYMENTS	$ _____
35 PAYMENT/INCOME RATIO (Use Line 33 Plus Line 34 For Income)	_____ %	49 MONTHLY DEPOSITS TO IMPOUND ACCOUNTS FOR TAXES AND INSURANCE	1 ☐ Yes 2 ☐ No
36 33% OF LINE 28	$ _____	50 PROPERTY IS INTENDED TO BE THE PRIMARY RESIDENCE OF BORROWER OR CO-BORROWER	1 ☐ Yes 2 ☐ No
37 OBLIGATIONS/INCOME RATIO (Use Line 33 Plus Line 36 For Income)	_____ %		

38A	38B SATELLITE MORTGAGE ORGANIZATION

SELLER'S RECOMMENDATION

WE, THE UNDERSIGNED, HAVE UNDERWRITTEN AND RECOMMEND THAT YOU [☐ APPROVE / ☐ PURCHASE] THE SUBMISSION DESCRIBED ABOVE IN ACCORDANCE WITH THE TERMS OF OUR OUTSTANDING FNMA SELLING CONTRACT.

SELLER'S NAME _____

SELLER/SERVICER NUMBER _____

SELLER'S ADDRESS _____

UNDERWRITER SIGNATURE _____

UNDERWRITER NAME _____   NUMBER _____

TITLE _____   DATE _____

APPRAISER NAME _____   NUMBER _____

FOR RESPONSE TO THIS SUBMISSION REFER TO SELLER'S LOAN NUMBER	PERSON TO CALL (If Other Than Underwriter)	SELLER'S TELEPHONE NUMBER

PREVIOUS EDITION MAY BE USED UNTIL STOCK IS EXHAUSTED   (C1)

FNMA Form 1008   Apr 80

IN ADDITION TO FNMA'S STANDARD DOCUMENTATION REQUIREMENTS, THE FOLLOWING EXHIBITS/COMMENTS ARE BEING FORWARDED IN SUPPORT OF THIS SUBMISSION:

EXHIBITS

A. _____
B. _____
C. _____
D) _____

UNDERWRITING CONSIDERATIONS

PROPERTY _____
_____
_____
_____
_____

MORTGAGOR APPLICANT(S) _____
_____
_____
_____

DELEGATED UNDERWRITING ONLY: SPECIAL CONDITIONS/REQUIREMENTS SELLER IMPOSED FOR LOAN APPROVAL
_____
_____
_____
_____
_____

UPON REVIEW OF THIS SUBMISSION

FNMA REVIEWER
(SIGNATURE) _____ REVIEWER NUMBER_____ ACTION DATE ___/___/___

A COMPLETED APPLICATION WAS RECEIVED BY FNMA ON _____
(DATE)

01☐ THE SUBMISSION HAS BEEN APPROVED.
　　SUBJECT TO THE FOLLOWING CONDITIONS:
　　1☐ SELLER MUST INCLUDE WITH DELIVERY APPRAISER'S CERTIFICATION THAT PROPERTY WAS COMPLETED IN ACCORDANCE WITH PLANS AND SPECIFICATIONS AS IDENTIFIED ON APPRAISAL REPORT.
　　2☐ SELLER MUST INCLUDE WITH DELIVERY ITS CERTIFICATION INDICATING REPAIRS TO THE PROPERTY AS STATED IN THE APPLICATION OR APPRAISAL REPORT HAVE BEEN SATISFACTORILY COMPLETED.
　　3☐ SELLER MUST INCLUDE WITH DELIVERY EVIDENCE THAT SALE OF BORROWER'S PREVIOUS RESIDENCE HAS BEEN COMPLETED, RESULTING IN NET PROCEEDS OF $_____.

　　4☐ OTHER: _____
_____
_____

02☐ THE SUBMISSION HAS BEEN RETURNED AT YOUR REQUEST
　☐ THE SUBMISSION HAS BEEN DECLINED FOR THE REASON(S) STATED BELOW.

CREDIT
03☐ NO CREDIT FILE
04☐ INSUFFICIENT CREDIT REFERENCES
05☐ INSUFFICIENT CREDIT FILE
06☐ UNABLE TO VERIFY CREDIT REFERENCES
07☐ GARNISHMENT, ATTACHMENT, FORECLOSURE, REPOSSESSION OR SUIT
08☐ INSUFFICIENT INCOME FOR TOTAL OBLIGATIONS
09☐ UNACCEPTABLE PAYMENT RECORD ON PREVIOUS MORTGAGE
10☐ LACK OF CASH RESERVES
11☐ DELINQUENT CREDIT OBLIGATIONS
12☐ BANKRUPTCY
　☐ INFORMATION FROM A CONSUMER REPORTING AGENCY
ADDITIONAL COMMENTS: _____
_____
_____
_____

EMPLOYMENT STATUS
19☐ UNABLE TO VERIFY EMPLOYMENT
20☐ LENGTH OF EMPLOYMENT
21☐ INSUFFICIENT STABILITY OF INCOME
INCOME
24☐ INSUFFICIENT INCOME FOR MORTGAGE PAYMENTS
25☐ UNABLE TO VERIFY INCOME
RESIDENCY
28☐ SECONDARY RESIDENCE
PROPERTY
33☐ UNACCEPTABLE PROPERTY
34☐ INSUFFICIENT DATA-PROPERTY
35☐ UNACCEPTABLE APPRAISAL
36☐ UNACCEPTABLE LEASEHOLD ESTATE
OTHER
37☐ INSUFFICIENT FUNDS TO CLOSE THE LOAN
38☐ CREDIT APPLICATION INCOMPLETE
39☐ WE DO NOT GRANT CREDIT TO ANY APPLICANT ON THE TERMS AND CONDITIONS YOU REQUEST

FNMA Form 1008 Apr 80

Appendix A—Part II
APPLICATION TO QUALIFY FOR FHA MORTGAGE

U.S. DEPARTMENT OF HOUSING AND URBAN DEVELOPMENT HOUSING – FEDERAL HOUSING COMMISSIONER **MORTGAGE CREDIT ANALYSIS WORKSHEET**	CASE NUMBER

SECTION I – LOAN DATA

1. NAME OF BORROWER AND CO-BORROWER	2. AMOUNT OF MORTGAGE $	3. CASH DOWN PAYMENT ON PURCHASE PRICE $

SECTION II – BORROWER'S/CO-BORROWER'S PERSONAL AND FINANCIAL STATUS

4. BORROW-ER'S AGE	5. OCCUPATION OF BORROWER		6. NO. OF YRS. AT PRESENT ADDRESS	7. ASSETS AVAILABLE FOR CLOSING	8. CURRENT MONTHLY RENTAL OR OTHER HOUSING EXPENSE
9. IS CO-BORROWER EMPLOYED?	10. CO-BORROWER'S AGE	11. OCCUPATION OF CO-BORROWER		12. NO. OF YEARS AT PRESENT EMPLOYMENT	13. OTHER DEPENDENTS (a) Ages _____ (b) Number _____

SECTION III – ESTIMATED MONTHLY SHELTER EXPENSES (This Property)

14. TERM OF LOAN (Months)	16. SETTLEMENT REQUIREMENTS

FUTURE MONTHLY PAYMENTS

15.			16.	
(a) Principal and Interest	$		(a) Existing Debt (Refinancing ONLY)	$
(b) FHA Mortgage Insurance Premium	$		(b) Sale Price (Realty ONLY)	$
(c) Ground Rent (Leasehold ONLY)	$		(c) Repairs and Improvements	$
(d) TOTAL DEBT SERVICE (A + B + C)	$		(d) Closing Costs	$
(e) Hazard Insurance	$		(e) TOTAL ACQUISITION COST (A + B + C + D)	$
(f) Taxes, Special Assessments	$		(f) Mortgage Amount	$
(g) TOTAL MTG. PAYMENT (D + E + F)	$		(g) Borrower(s)' Required Investment (E minus F)	$
(h) Maintenance and Common Expense	$		(h) Prepayable Expenses	$
(i) Heat and Utilities	$		(i) Non-Realty and Other Items	$
(j) TOTAL HSG. EXPENSE (G + H + I)	$		(j) TOTAL REQUIREMENTS (G + H + I)	$
(k) Other Recurring Charges (explain)	$		(k) Amount paid ☐ cash ☐ other (explain)	$
(l) TOTAL FIXED PAYMENT (j + K)	$		(l) Amt. to be paid ☐ cash ☐ other (explain)	$
			(m) TOTAL ASSETS AVAILABLE FOR CLOSING	$

SECTION IV – MONTHLY EFFECTIVE INCOME

SECTION V – DEBTS AND OBLIGATIONS

		ITEM	✓	Monthly Payment	Unpaid Balance
17. Borrower's Base Pay	$	25. State and Local Income Taxes		$	$
18. Other Earnings (explain)	$	26. Social Security/Retirement			
19. Co-Borrower's Base Pay	$	27.			
20. Other Earnings (explain)	$	28.			
21. Income, Real Estate	$	29.			
22. TOTAL MONTHLY EFFECTIVE INCOME	$	30.			
23. Less Federal Tax	$	31.			
24. NET EFFECTIVE INCOME	$	32.			

SECTION VI – BORROWER RATING

33.		TOTAL	$	$

34. Borrower Rating		39. FINAL	SECTION VII-RATIOS	40. ☐ Loan to Value Ratio _____ %	43. ☐ Ratio of Net Effective Income to:
35. Credit Characteristics		☐ Approve Application			Total Housing Expense _____ %
36. Adequacy of Eff. Income				41. Total Payment to Rental Value _____ %	
37. Stability of Eff. Income		☐ Reject Application		42. Debt Service to Rental Income _____ %	Total Fixed Payment _____ %
38. Adequacy of Available Assets					

44. REMARKS (Use reverse, if necessary)   First Time Home Buyer? ☐ Yes ☐ No

45. SIGNATURE OF EXAMINER	46. DATE

RETAIN ORIGINAL IN CASE BINDER, FORWARD COPY TO MANAGEMENT INFORMATION SYSTEMS DIVISION WITH HUD-92900-8

HUD-92900-WS (5-81)

Appendix A—Part III
APPLICATION TO QUALIFY FOR A VA MORTGAGE

LOAN ANALYSIS		LOAN NUMBER

SECTION A–LOAN DATA

1 NAME OF BORROWER	2 AMOUNT OF LOAN	3 CASH DOWN PAYMENT ON PURCHASE PRICE
	$	$

SECTION B–BORROWER'S PERSONAL AND FINANCIAL STATUS

4 APPLICANT'S AGE	5 OCCUPATION OF APPLICANT		6 NUMBER OF YEARS AT PRESENT EMPLOYMENT	7 LIQUID ASSETS (Cash, savings bonds, etc.)	8 CURRENT MONTHLY RENTAL OR OTHER HOUSING EXPENSE
				$	$
9 IS SPOUSE EMPLOYED? ☐ YES ☐ NO	10 SPOUSE'S AGE	11 OCCUPATION OF SPOUSE		12 NUMBER OF YEARS AT PRESENT EMPLOYMENT	13 AGE OF OTHER DEPENDENTS

SECTION C – ESTIMATED MONTHLY SHELTER EXPENSES (This Property) / SECTION D – DEBTS AND OBLIGATIONS (Itemize and indicate by (√) which debts considered in Section E, Line 41)

	ITEMS	AMOUNT		ITEMS	(√)	MO. PAYMENT	UNPAID BAL.
14	TERM OF LOAN YEARS		23			$	$
15	MORTGAGE PAYMENT (Principal and Interest)	$	24				
16	REALTY TAXES		25				
17	HAZARD INSURANCE		26				
18	SPECIAL ASSESSMENTS		27				
19	MAINTENANCE		28				
20	UTILITIES (Including heat)		29				
21	OTHER		30	JOB RELATED EXPENSE (Child care, etc.)			
22	TOTAL	$	31	TOTAL		$	$

SECTION E – MONTHLY INCOME AND DEDUCTIONS

	ITEMS		SPOUSE	BORROWER	TOTAL
32	GROSS SALARY OR EARNINGS FROM EMPLOYMENT		$	$	$
33	DEDUCTIONS	FEDERAL INCOME TAX			
34		STATE INCOME TAX			
35		RETIREMENT OR SOCIAL SECURITY			
36		OTHER (Specify)			
37		TOTAL DEDUCTIONS	$	$	$
38	NET TAKE HOME PAY				
39	PENSION COMPENSATION OR OTHER NET INCOME (Specify)				
40	TOTAL (Sum of lines 38 and 39)		$	$	$
41	LESS THOSE OBLIGATIONS LISTED IN SECTION D WHICH SHOULD BE DEDUCTED FROM INCOME				
42	TOTAL NET EFFECTIVE INCOME				$
43	LESS ESTIMATED MONTHLY SHELTER EXPENSE (Line 22)				
44	BALANCE AVAILABLE FOR FAMILY SUPPORT				$

45 PAST CREDIT RECORD ☐ SATISFACTORY ☐ UNSATISFACTORY	46 DOES LOAN MEET VA CREDIT STANDARDS? (Give reasons for decision under "Remarks," if necessary, e.g., borderline case) ☐ YES ☐ NO

47 REMARKS (Use reverse, if necessary)

SECTION F – DISPOSITION OF APPLICATION

☐ Recommend that the application be approved since it meets all requirements of Chapter 37, Title 38, U.S. Code and applicable VA Regulations and directives.

☐ Recommend that the application be disapproved for the reasons stated under "Remarks" above.

48 DATE	49 SIGNATURE OF EXAMINER	
50 FINAL ACTION ☐ APPROVE APPLICATION ☐ REJECT APPLICATION	51 DATE	52 SIGNATURE AND TITLE OF APPROVING OFFICIAL

VA FORM 26-6393 (1443)
AUG 1975

EXISTING STOCK OF VA FORM 26-6393, SEP 1974 WILL BE USED

APPENDIX B
GOOD FAITH ESTIMATE OF SETTLEMENT COSTS

Colonial Name

Branch Office Address

Telephone Number

GOOD FAITH ESTIMATE OF SETTLEMENT COSTS

APPLICANT(S) _____ DATE _____

PROPERTY ADDRESS _____

SALES PRICE _____ LOAN AMOUNT _____

NOTICE – THIS FORM DOES NOT COVER ALL ITEMS YOU WILL BE REQUIRED TO PAY IN CASH AT SETTLEMENT, FOR EXAMPLE, DEPOSIT IN ESCROW FOR REAL ESTATE TAXES AND INSURANCE. YOU MAY WISH TO INQUIRE AS TO THE AMOUNT OF OTHER SUCH ITEMS. YOU MAY BE REQUIRED TO PAY OTHER ADDITIONAL AMOUNTS AT SETTLEMENT

THIS GOOD FAITH ESTIMATE OF SETTLEMENT COSTS IS MADE PURSUANT TO THE REQUIREMENTS OF THE REAL ESTATE SETTLEMENT PROCEDURES ACT. THESE FIGURES ARE ONLY ESTIMATES AND THE ACTUAL CHARGES DUE AT SETTLEMENT MAY BE DIFFERENT.

L. SETTLEMENT CHARGES		
800. ITEMS PAYABLE IN CONNECTION WITH THE LOAN		**AMOUNT**
801.	Loan Origination Fee %	$
802.	Loan Discount %	
803.	Appraisal Fee	
804.	Credit Report Fee	
805.	Lender's Inspection Fee	
806.	Mortgage Insurance Application Fee	
807.	Assumption Fee	
808.	Application Fee	
809.	VA Funding Fee	
810.	HUD Mortgage Insurance Premium	
811.		
900. ITEMS REQUIRED BY LENDER TO BE PAID IN ADVANCE		
901.	Interest from to @ /day	
902.	Mortgage Insurance Premium for months to	
1100. TITLE CHARGES		
1101.	Settlement or closing fee	
1102.	Abstract or Title search	
1103.	Title Examination	
1104.	Title Insurance Binder	
1105.	Document Preparation	
1106.	Notary Fees	
1107.	Attorney's fees (including above items numbers;)	
1108.	Title Insurance (including above items numbers;)	
1109.	Lender's Coverage	
1110.	Owner's Coverage	
1111.	Endorsement(s):	
1112.		
1200. GOVERNMENT RECORDING AND TRANSFER CHARGES		
1201.	Recording Fees: Deed $ Mortgage $ Release $	
1202.	City/County Tax/Stamps Deed $ Mortgage $	
1203.	State Tax/Stamps Deed $ Mortgage $	
1204.		
1300. ADDITIONAL SETTLEMENT CHARGES		
1301.	Survey	
1302.	Pest Inspection	
1303.	Amortization Schedule	
1304.		
1305.		
TOTAL ESTIMATED SETTLEMENT CHARGES		$

I HEREBY ACKNOWLEDGE THAT I HAVE RECEIVED A COPY OF THIS GOOD FAITH ESTIMATE OF SETTLEMENT COSTS AND A COPY OF THE HUD GUIDE FOR HOME BUYERS "SETTLEMENT COSTS AND YOU".

_____ _____ _____ _____
APPLICANT'S SIGNATURE   DATE   APPLICANT'S SIGNATURE   DATE

IF MAILED, BY: _____
                                                        DATE

(G15A)

Appendix C

L. SETTLEMENT CHARGES	PAID FROM BORROWER'S FUNDS	PAID FROM SELLER'S FUNDS
700. SALES BROKER'S COMMISSION based on price $ @ %		
701. Total commission paid by seller		
Division of commission as follows:		
702. $ to		
703. $ to		
704.		
800. ITEMS PAYABLE IN CONNECTION WITH LOAN		
801. Loan Origination fee %		
802. Loan Discount %		
803. Appraisal Fee to		
804. Credit Report to		
805. Lender's inspection fee		
806. Mortgage Insurance application fee to		
807. Assumption fee		
808.		
809.		
810.		
811.		
900. ITEMS REQUIRED BY LENDER TO BE PAID IN ADVANCE.		
901. Interest from to @ $ /day		
902. Mortgage insurance premium for mo. to		
903. Hazard insurance premium for yrs. to		
904.		
905.		
1000. RESERVES DEPOSITED WITH LENDER FOR:		
1001. Hazard insurance mo. @ $ /mo.		
1002. Mortgage insurance mo. @ $ /mo.		
1003. City property taxes mo. @ $ /mo.		
1004. County property taxes mo. @ $ /mo.		
1005. Annual assessments mo. @ $ /mo.		
1006. mo. @ $ /mo.		
1007.		
1008.		
1100. TITLE CHARGES:		
1101. Settlement or closing fee to		
1102. Abstract or title search to		
1103. Title examination to		
1104. Title insurance binder to		
1105. Document preparation to		
1106. Notary fees to		
1107. Attorney's Fees to		
(includes above items No.:		
1108. Title insurance to		
(includes above items No.:		
1109. Lender's coverage $		
1110. Owner's coverage $		
1111.		
1112.		
1113.		
1200. GOVERNMENT RECORDING AND TRANSFER CHARGES		
1201. Recording fees: Deed $; Mortgage $ Release $		
1202.		
1203. State tax/stamps: Deed $ to:		
1204.		
1300. ADDITIONAL SETTLEMENT CHARGES		
1301. Survey to		
1302. Pest inspection to		
1303.		
1304.		
1305.		
1400. TOTAL SETTLEMENT CHARGES (entered on lines 103 and 503, Sections J and K)		

NOTE: Under certain circumstances the borrower and seller may be permitted to waive the 12-day period which must normally occur between advance disclosure and settlement. In the event such a waiver is made, copies of the statements of waiver, executed as provided in the regulations of the Department of Housing and Urban Development, shall be attached to and made a part of this form when the form is used as a settlement statement.

	Seller			Purchaser
	Seller			Purchaser
Address		Address		

83

INDEX

About the Authors

PHYLLIS C. KAUFMAN, the originator of the No Nonsense Guides, is a Philadelphia attorney and theatrical producer. A graduate of Brandeis University, she was an editor of the law review at Temple University School of Law. She is listed in *Who's Who in American Law*, *Who's Who of American Women*, *Who's Who in Finance and Industry*, and *Foremost Women of the Twentieth Century*.

ARNOLD CORRIGAN, noted financial expert, is the author of *How Your IRA Can Make You a Millionaire* and is a frequent guest on financial talk shows. A senior officer of a large New York investment advisory firm, he holds Bachelor's and Master's degrees in economics from Harvard and has written for *Barron's* and other financial publications.